P9-ARC-513

in the french kitchen with kids

in the french kitchen with kids

Easy, everyday dishes for
the whole family to make and enjoy

Mardi Michels

appetite
by RANDOM HOUSE

Copyright © 2018 Mardi Michels

All rights reserved. The use of any part of this publication, reproduced, transmitted in any form or by any means electronic, mechanical, photocopying, recording or otherwise, or stored in a retrieval system without the prior written consent of the publisher—or in the case of photocopying or other reprographic copying, license from the Canadian Copyright Licensing Agency—is an infringement of the copyright law.

Appetite by Random House™ and colophon are registered trademarks of Penguin Random House LLC.

Library and Archives of Canada Cataloguing in Publication is available upon request.

ISBN: 978-0-14-753077-6
eBook ISBN: 978-0-14-753078-3

Photography by Kyla Zanardi, except for photos on pages viii, 2, 22, 53, 56, 82, 104, 116, 122, 145, 162, 169, 172, 173 and 174 by Mardi Michels
Food styling by Dara Sutin, except for cover photo styled by Mardi Michels
Illustrations by Lisa Orgler

Printed and bound in China

Published in Canada by Appetite by Random House™, a division of Penguin Random House LLC.

www.penguinrandomhouse.ca

10 9 8 7 6 5

for mum,
who taught me how to cook.

for dad,
who encouraged me to write.

♡

contents

FLUTE
7
CEREALES
1€50

FICELL
0€80

FOREWORD *by dorie greenspan*

Reading Mardi's book, it was impossible not to think of this well-worn proverb: Give a man a fish and you feed him for a day. Teach a man to fish and you feed him for a lifetime. It's true that if you learn to feed yourself, you'll never be hungry. But learning to cook goes far beyond the elemental. I believe this deeply and I know it personally and practically.

I didn't learn to cook until I had to, which was when I got married and took on the responsibility of feeding myself and my husband. At that time, all I wanted to do was get a meal on the table without mishap—and I wasn't always successful. It's a good thing the pottery dish I put over a direct flame didn't hurt anyone when it cracked—no one was hit by the shards or the boiling water, and the frozen peas weren't really needed for dinner anyway.

Teaching myself to cook was frustrating for a while . . . and then it wasn't. Once the fear of failure (if not a missed meal) subsided, I began to understand what it means to cook. There's the enjoyment in the work itself: whether chopping, blending or baking, the basic actions of transforming ingredients touches all our senses. I still smile whenever I see my ingredients lined up on the counter, ready to be turned into something good. There's the satisfaction of being competent, the fundamental pride when we know there's a job to be done and that we can do it. And there's the pleasure, the wonderful sense of joy, when we share what we've cooked with people we love.

It took me years to come to this. The lucky boys in Mardi's *Les Petits Chefs* club, and you, the lucky readers of this book, don't have to wait. You now have everything you need to set yourself and your children on the path to a lifetime of happiness in the kitchen.

There are many people who are passionate about food; some are knowledgeable as well. What is rare is to find a person who cares and knows about food and who can pass that along. Mardi is that rare person. That she is generous and shares everything she knows is our good fortune.

I have followed the progress of Mardi and her Petits Chefs for years now. I have delighted at what they've cooked—I admit to melting every time I see a picture of those little fingers crimping dough or scooping cookies. And I've marveled at the complexity of what they've done. As Mardi says of her students, they have a "can-do" attitude. They have it because they're young and they don't know what's supposed to be too difficult for them. And they have it because Mardi encourages them to have it. As this book proves, French home cooking is simple, nourishing and absolutely doable for kids.

Here's to more good food from more *petits chefs*. Merci, Mardi.

INTRODUCTION

Twice a week during school terms, our school science lab takes on a bit of a different look. If you look in, you'll see about a dozen boys slicing, dicing, mixing, kneading, sprinkling and tasting, the evidence of their "experiments" all over the lab benches. Yet, unlikely as the setting may be, what is taking place in the lab is a cooking class that's now been running since 2010.

In 2005 I started teaching French at an all-boys school, where one of my responsibilities was—and still is—to run an after-school club. Initially I offered technology-based clubs, taking advantage of the resources we had available and, of course, catering to the boys' interests. But in the fall of 2009, I heard Jamie Oliver speak in Toronto about the Food Revolution and his "Pass It On" campaign, which focused on getting people back into the kitchen and cooking. Throughout his talk, all I could think about was that I, an educator, had a duty to contribute to this campaign in some way. I knew I wanted to pass on my knowledge and love of cooking, and with the opportunity for a new after-school club before me, it seemed like the time was right to try something new! I figured that it would not only teach my students valuable life skills, but also be a great way for me to get to know them (and them, me) outside the classroom, doing something I really loved. French as a Second Language is not always everyone's favorite subject, and I was excited by this chance to show the boys another side of me! I put the idea to my boss, and the next thing I knew, I was standing in a science lab with 15 boys, aged between 9 and 12, eager to learn how to cook (and me, a little like a deer in the headlights!).

The past few years have been quite the learning experience, both for the boys and for me. One thing that has become extremely clear to me is that kids CAN cook and that they love it. When I first started teaching cooking, I used recipes I thought would be simple to make in less-than-ideal conditions in under an hour. While I was spot-on with my assessment of those recipes, somewhere around Week 4 of the club I realized the boys were whipping through the recipes and that they were too easy. And the boys were getting bored. I switched to using *Jamie's Food Revolution* cookbook with them, and I immediately saw much more engagement. The recipes, though still basic, were ones that would be invaluable resources for growing boys who would be cooking for themselves in a few years. Sure, we made burgers and pizza, but we made them from scratch. I have no problem with the boys learning how to make their favorite takeout or store-bought foods, because if it tastes good and they know how easy it is, they might be more likely to make it themselves than to buy less nutritionally rich takeout or store-bought versions.

Over the years, the cooking club evolved to be more than just cooking with me. I've introduced a guest program where local chefs and food enthusiasts work with the boys, either in our lab or in their restaurant kitchens. The boys have had the chance to work in some of the finest kitchens in Toronto (and beyond). They've cooked on *Breakfast Television Toronto*, one of Canada's top morning shows. A few boys were invited to hear René Redzepi, of the famed noma restaurant, speak. Outside of school, one of the boys even hosted his own pop-up dinner at a community kitchen (gnocchi from scratch for 30? No problem!) because he saw no issue with an 11-year-old taking that on.

But alongside these "big" opportunities, I like to celebrate the smaller rewards that come with teaching kids to cook. The emails with photos of the boys cooking at home; photos of a cooking class a boy has taken on my recommendation in Paris; a takeout container of a home-cooked meal that a boy has made for his family, ensuring he's made enough to bring me a serving the next day—along with a menu he's written up; the parent-teacher interviews where most of the allotted time is spent talking about cooking club; the *"Ça va bien parce qu'il y a le club de cuisine après l'école aujourd'hui"* ("I'm great because cooking club is after school today") I hear so often in class when I ask how someone's day is going.

There is a lot of joy in teaching kids to cook, but sometimes I'm so focused on getting everyone out the door on time that I don't stop to take in all that we've accomplished. That we made pastry from scratch, and then we made quiches, and then while they were baking, we made more pastry and cleaned up, for example. In 60 minutes. But when I'm dismissing the boys and I stop to breathe, I look at their faces and I get it. Just like the parents when they pick up their boys. What's going on is joy, creativity and, most of all, learning.

One of the greatest pleasures of teaching kids to cook comes from working with their can-do attitude, which has encouraged me in my own baking and cooking to just "have a go." The boys NEVER think something can't be done unless they've been told it's supposed to be hard. Puff pastry? Choux pastry? Sushi? Molecular cuisine? Working alongside some of the country's top chefs? No problem for kids who believe they can do anything.

Teaching kids cooking is also about embracing their natural confidence and making them feel that anything is possible. That they can cook.

So, why a French cookbook for kids? Well, France is a country dear to my heart. I lived there for years in my late 20s and have been back countless times since I moved to Canada from my native Australia. We own a little house in southwest France, so a part of me is always there. I love writing about French culture and the French language. And, of course, I love teaching kids to cook, and I am always on the lookout for ways to incorporate a little cooking into the French as a Second Language curriculum because, well, *pourquoi pas?* As I've watched my cooking club evolve over the years to include more complex recipes that many people don't think kids are capable of making (with a little help, of course!), the idea for this book was born. Kids can cook French food! Because despite what many people think, French food is not all sophisticated haute cuisine. At home, French people eat and cook mostly simple dishes. Dishes I know my cooking club members would love to make and eat. This book features real French food for kids, a little bit of culture, and some French language lessons too! I hope to take the intimidation factor out of French food through recipes for everyday dishes that children and their parents can make and eat together. Because you know what? Kids can cook. You just have to let them!

Bon appétit!

Mardi

top tips for cooking with kids

Do you like the idea of cooking with your kids but don't know where to start? It's nice to think you might just wander into the kitchen and start cooking with your kids, but you do need to be somewhat organized. A little bit of planning will not only help your cooking session run smoothly but also model organizational skills in the kitchen that will set your child on the road to working more independently.

Remember, though, when you're starting out, cooking with kids isn't always pretty. If you follow me on Instagram or read my blog, you'll be familiar with those kids' cooking photos I share weekly. Even though these are not staged, I choose what I share. This means that for every adorable photo of little hands rolling pastry perfectly, there are ten others of little hands playing with pastry, giant messes of flour all over countertops or the floor and others showing what can only be described as "organized chaos." So, if your kitchen is a little messy the first few times, know that it's totally normal! "What about injuries?" I hear you say. Well, we've had our fair share of cut and grated fingers, jalapeño fingers rubbed in eyes and burns from hot plates. Again, real life. Just make sure you know what to do and teach your children what to do if someone gets hurt. Ready to get started? Before you head to the kitchen with your kids (and even without them!) here are a few simple tips to ensure you are set up for success.

1. Read your recipe! Read the recipe all the way through a couple of times. Make sure you understand the instructions and have all the ingredients and equipment required. You might think this is common sense, but too many times I've found myself missing an important ingredient or a piece of equipment mid-recipe. Or I've miscalculated the amount of time a recipe will take from start to finish (note that some of the recipes in this book need to be prepped the day before you will actually eat them). There may be terms in the recipe that you need to clarify for your little chefs. You'll find that if you do this every time you cook together, you'll need to explain less and less each time.

2. Organize your *mise en place.*

Mise en what? It's a French term meaning to put everything in its place. This has two parts—gathering the ingredients and equipment, and then prepping all the ingredients so you are ready to bake, cook and assemble. I suggest placing the ingredients and equipment on the countertop in the order in which you will need them. This is another way of checking you have everything you need before you get started. Now, prep your ingredients. This is where small metal or ceramic prep bowls (the dollar store is your friend) come in very handy. By chopping, dicing, measuring or weighing all the ingredients you will need before you start cooking, you'll save time in the long run. In the ingredients lists, I've indicated where you need to peel or chop something as part of your *mise en place.*

3. Demonstrate, don't do.

Kids are remarkably capable in the kitchen, but they need to be shown how to do certain things, sometimes multiple times, before they can work on their own. You can start a task to show them how—but let them have a go! My students regularly demonstrate excellent knife skills, but did they always know what they were doing? Not at all—but they learn fast if they are given the chance to practice. So don't take that away from them by taking over.

4. Mistakes are okay! Life would be

very boring if no one made mistakes, wouldn't it? When you're cooking with kids, let them make mistakes (as in, stand back and let them get on with it unless there is some imminent danger). It's hard to give up control, especially if you are in a hurry or if you can see a dish really isn't going to turn out, but kids won't learn unless they are allowed to make mistakes. Let them know it's okay, and even necessary. Mistakes give you the opportunity to talk about what went wrong and why, and also discuss how you can salvage something that didn't quite go to plan.

5. Be flexible and patient.

As I mentioned above, when you're cooking with kids, sometimes things don't quite go according to plan. Look at these as teachable moments. Rolled your dough out a little too thin? Are you still able to work with it? If so, how will you adjust the baking time? If not, can it be re-rolled to the correct thickness? Most times, mistakes can be fixed, and it's important to show kids how to salvage a recipe, but you have to be prepared for the possibility that a recipe might not look quite as it was intended to. And remember, your idea of what something is supposed to look like is probably vastly different than a child's! In the kitchen with kids, remember that patience is a virtue. Anyone who has cooked with their child will know that everything takes much longer. Just remember, the more you cook with kids, the more efficient they will become. Be patient. Resist the urge to take over because it will be faster. Factor in extra time to prepare even the easiest recipe when you first start cooking with kids and eventually that extra time won't be necessary.

If you do have the chance to cook with children, I urge you to snap up that chance immediately. As well as teaching them valuable life skills, it's so rewarding and it can even teach you to be more organized and efficient in the kitchen.

IN THE FRENCH PANTRY

When you hear the expression "French food," you might think you'll need to stock your pantry with all sorts of high-end ingredients. You'll be pleased to know this is not the case. A lot of people associate anything French with haute cuisine, and while there is definitely a level of French cuisine that is restaurant-only fare, the food most French people eat tends to be much simpler. When you take a closer look at some of the dishes featured in this book, you will realize that the techniques and recipes themselves are much simpler than you expected and that only very occasionally is a special ingredient or piece of equipment called for. You may notice that the same basic pantry and fridge staples appear in many of the recipes, meaning that a lot of these dishes can even be made on a whim. Where a recipe calls for a more unusual ingredient, I've made a note of this and given suggestions for where to buy it or for a substitute.

butter

Recipes in this book use either salted or unsalted butter—they are not interchangeable. The recipe for Quick Croissants (p. 27) works best with European-style butter, which has a higher fat content (less water) than our everyday North American butter. Look for something with 83% or more fat. In a recipe for something like croissants it will make a big difference, but rest assured the recipe works with regular salted butter too. The ingredients list will tell you if the butter should be cold, room temperature or melted to help you plan. If you've forgotten to bring your butter to room temperature, don't be tempted to pop it into the microwave. Instead, measure or weigh the butter you'll need, cut it into tiny pieces and place it in a single layer on a large plate or tray. Within about 30 minutes, it will be at the right temperature for you to use.

milk

These recipes have been tested with both whole (3.25%) and part-skim (2%) milk. Do not use skim (1% or 0%) milk, because it will affect the end product in baked goods (you're essentially changing the fat content).

cream

Heavy cream in this book means whipping cream (35%). For cooking, you can substitute table cream (18%) but the result won't be quite the same.

(In the topping for the Shepherd's Pie (p. 89), for example, heavy cream produces a silky mashed potato; a lighter cream or—heaven forbid!—skim milk will not.)

eggs

The recipes in this book use large eggs that weigh around 2 oz (60 g). Eggs in the baking recipes will always be used at room temperature. If you forget to take your eggs out in time, place them in a bowl of lukewarm water and let them sit for a couple of minutes. Drain them, add fresh lukewarm water and let them sit for a couple more minutes. *Voilà*—now you have room-temperature eggs!

flour

Most recipes in this book use all-purpose (plain) flour. Please note that I have not tested the recipes with any gluten-free flours.

For baking, I weigh my flour but if you don't own a digital scale (buy one!), you can measure your flour in cups. When I am cooking with kids and using a recipe that calls for volume measures for dry ingredients, I put a little more flour than we are going to need in a large bowl and "fluff" it up with a fork or a whisk. (If you are not cooking with kids, you can simply fluff the flour in the package so that it is not tightly packed as you are trying to scoop it.) Dip the cup measure into the flour and take a scoop. There should be more than your cup measure—take the flat side of a butter knife and, pushing the flour away from you (over the bowl or package), level it off.

sugar

The recipes in this book use three types of sugar—granulated sugar, icing sugar and brown sugar. They are not interchangeable, and each recipe specifies which one to use. You'll also see some recipes call for pearl sugar, a coarse sugar that does not melt when baked and is typically used to decorate breads (*Gâteau des rois brioché* on p. 153, for example) or pastries (*Chouquettes* on p. 61, for example). You can buy it at some baking supply stores or online.

salt

For baking, I use fine sea salt. For cooking and seasoning, flaky sea salt is my preferred choice.

yeast

Two different types of yeast are used in this book—active dry and instant (or rapid rise). These are not interchangeable, as they are prepared and interact with various ingredients differently. Be sure to use the yeast that is specified.

chocolate

Most of the recipes in this book that use chocolate have been tested with standard chocolate chips (they are easy to weigh and measure) or baking chocolate. That said, use the best-quality chocolate you can afford, because there are very few ingredients in many of the recipes, so quality does make a difference. The Pains au chocolat (p. 63) use chocolate baking sticks, which you can find at specialty baking stores.

almond meal

Many French dessert and cake recipes call for almond meal (also sold as "almond flour"), which is finely ground, blanched (skin removed) almonds that you can buy pre-ground. You can also make this by grinding almonds yourself in a spice or coffee grinder (make sure it's well rinsed before you use it for your almonds). I find it's easiest to purchase pre-ground almond meal, as I always end up with near–almond butter when I grind it myself! Nuts.com sells an excellent, very finely ground almond meal, if you are looking to buy a larger (5 lb/2.25 kg) quantity, and it keeps well in an airtight container in the freezer. Otherwise, Bob's Red Mill is a reliable choice.

produce

As well as listing the quantity and approximate size of fruits and vegetables used, I've also included the approximate weight. You will have a much higher chance of success if you consistently follow the weights listed in the recipes. "Really?" I hear you ask. Yes, really. I challenge you to go shopping with a group of friends (or kids!) and have everyone shop for one large carrot, one medium yellow onion and three small apples. Now, go to a farmers' market and do the same thing. I can guarantee that no two people will have produce weighing the same amount. In some recipes (like the Creamy Vegetable Soup, p. 43) it doesn't matter so much. In others (like the Quick Stovetop Ratatouille, p. 107) it will make a big difference. There are scales in many supermarkets to help you with this task.

For kids, part of the fun of cooking can also be the shopping, so try to make weighing ingredients an integral part of your shopping trips. At a farmers' market, you can even ask for ingredients by weight.

EQUIPMENT IN THE FRENCH KITCHEN

People often tell me that they couldn't possibly attempt a French recipe (especially with kids), because it must surely require special equipment. As you saw in the ingredients section, French pantry and fridge staples are anything but fancy, and the same can be said for equipment.

The recipes in this book have been tested all over the world, in kitchens of all degrees of sophistication, from the most basic to the best equipped. A lot of these recipes were even tested in the science lab at school, where we have only the essentials but were still able to achieve excellent results.

It's important, especially in baking, to be able to touch and feel, as well as see, ingredients transform before your eyes. With choux pastry, for example, many recipes call for using a stand mixer (which we don't have at school) or handheld electric beaters (which we do). I teach the boys how to make choux by hand, with a bowl and a wooden spoon to mix the eggs into the dough, and they do just fine. By making pastries and doughs by hand the first few times, little (and not so little) bakers can get a good idea of how the dough is supposed to feel at each stage of the recipe. If you make a recipe entirely by hand a few times, you'll be in a better position to judge "readiness" once you start using a mixer or food processor.

In terms of making sure your kitchen is equipped with the right tools to make these recipes, I'm in a good position to advise. We recently bought a house in southwest France that we rent out as a holiday home. When we took possession, it was literally an empty shell of a house—a blank slate. When it came to furnishing and equipping the house, we found ourselves questioning every purchase; the house is small, so we don't want clutter. What we ended up with is one of the best-equipped vacation rental kitchens we've seen (and we've seen a lot) and an excellent "basics" list that has helped streamline the equipment used in these recipes. I was developing these recipes over a few different trips to France so the "must have" equipment list stemmed from what I needed then. In this book, where a recipe calls for a special piece of equipment, I've made a note of this at the beginning of the recipe.

Here's my list of equipment basics, with some optional extras.

MEASURING

digital scale

Once considered a tool for professionals rather than home cooks, these are now commonly found in kitchens all over the world. There is no better way to measure ingredients than to weigh them. I've watched as the boys in my cooking club each measured 1 cup (150 g) of flour using dry cup measures. Not one of those cups was the same weight—and in some cases, the difference was about 1 oz (more than 20 g) per cup. This can make a huge difference, especially in baking, so while I do provide cup measures, I cook and bake nearly exclusively by weight nowadays (and yes, the digital scale was one of the first items I purchased for our French kitchen).

As I explained in the pantry section, I've even listed approximate weight for fruits and vegetables because I can bet that my idea of a "small yellow onion" is different from yours. Using the right amount of ingredients in a recipe is the key to success and now, for around $20, you can purchase a digital kitchen scale that will make a huge difference. Kids LOVE using the scale (they actually fight over that task in my cooking club!), so take advantage of their enthusiasm and embrace cooking and baking by weight.

measuring cups and spoons

You'll need a set of cup measures for dry ingredients, especially if you are not going to use a scale. Measuring spoons are needed for smaller quantities of dry ingredients as well as for measuring some liquids. If budget and space permit, it's nice to have two sets of each so you don't need to wash equipment halfway through a recipe.

liquid measures

You'll need glass measuring jugs to measure liquid in these recipes. Make sure the jug is on a level surface when you pour the liquid in and that you are at eye level with it. Coincidentally, this happens to be a perfect job for kids! I also like to use jugs to pour larger quantities of liquids (custards, etc.) into smaller dishes like ramekins; it makes for much less mess!

KITCHEN UTENSILS

wooden spoons

Have a variety of wooden spoons available so you don't have to wash them mid-recipe.

heat-resistant rubber or silicone spatulas

I like to use spatulas to fold dry ingredients into wet ingredients because it reminds me to be gentle. With baking, dry ingredients should be folded in only until they are just combined with the wet ones (to avoid over-mixing). I find that when I give kids a wooden spoon, they stir and stir with great enthusiasm and so sometimes over-mix. A spatula feels a little different, more delicate. You're also going to need one to scrape your batter or dough into its baking pan, so it also means less washing up if you're already using it to mix that batter or dough.

offset spatula

An offset spatula is useful for removing rolled-out cookies from parchment or baked cookies from trays to cool, flattening croquettes (p. 103 and p. 111), smoothing cream onto pastry (p. 143) or even frosting cakes.

wire (balloon) whisk

These are useful for blending dry ingredients together and for adding volume to liquid ingredients like eggs. You might consider buying a smaller whisk that fits in a glass measuring jug and a larger one to use in bigger bowls.

bench scrapers (plastic or metal)

A bench scraper is generally a metal tool that helps you lift rolled-out dough or pastry off a work surface while keeping it together. It's also good for cutting dough and pastry disks, and for scraping off a work surface to clean it—just make sure your work surface can handle a metal blade. If you're working on a softer surface that can't take a metal blade, you can buy plastic bench scrapers that are not as sturdy but do get the job done. You can use these to scrape batter out of mixing bowls as well.

pastry blender

Some of the dough and pastry recipes in this book call for "cutting" butter into flour. A pastry blender, which can be purchased at any baking supply store, is a handheld tool with thin metal strips attached to a handle. You hold the handle and press the metal strips into the butter and flour, and it helps break the large pieces of butter into smaller pieces, mixing the flour in at the same time. Many people love this tool but, to be honest, I've had one for only a very short time—I usually use my fingertips to rub the butter into the flour (or use a food processor).

pastry brushes

Lots of the recipes call for egg wash, which is easiest to apply with a small pastry brush. These look like paint brushes and can be purchased at any baking supply store.

SMALL APPLIANCES

food processor

While I do suggest that most tasks in this book can be completed by hand, there are a lot of jobs where using the food processor can save time (and mess, although I'd argue that making a mess is all part of cooking with kids!) and/or is recommended for maximum success with the recipe. The Trio of Salads (pp. 54, 55 and 57), the Crunchy Fish Cakes (p. 103), the Crispy Vegetable Cakes (p. 111) and most of the pastry recipes (pp. 164–175) certainly benefit from the help of a food processor.

handheld electric beaters

Handheld electric beaters are useful for making batter and dough and for whipping egg whites and cream. All the recipes in this book were tested, and can be prepared, using this relatively inexpensive stand mixer alternative. I like handheld beaters for many reasons, but especially because in recipes like the *Cœur à la crème* (pp. 119 and 121) you can prepare all your ingredients in separate bowls with no need to rinse the beater attachments (or bowls) in between steps.

immersion blender

Useful for puréeing soups, although blenders and some food processors can do this now too.

stand mixer

If you already have a stand mixer, great! As they are more powerful than handheld electric beaters, you'll likely save some time using one. If you bake regularly, it's probably wise to invest in some extra bowls to avoid mid-recipe washing up.

BOWLS AND DISHES

bowls

I have a range of mixing bowls in varying sizes and materials—metal, ceramic and plastic. Smaller metal bowls can be used for your *mise en place*, and I strongly recommend a trip to the dollar store to buy a bunch of these.

a scrap bowl (always!)

Something I've learned to make an essential part of any *mise en place* is a scrap and/or garbage bowl. Usually I have one for food scraps and another for non-organic waste (packaging, etc.). I find it helps immensely with cleanup and encourages kids to work in a tidy environment.

FOR BAKING

For the recipes in this book, you'll need:

✓ 2 x baking trays (metal, with rims). I like to use lighter-colored metal rimmed baking trays (I have half-sheet pans that are 18 x 13 inches/45 x 33 cm, so slightly larger than a regular cookie sheet). I find the lighter metal conducts heat more evenly than the darker nonstick cookie sheets, so while they are a little more expensive, they are a worthwhile investment. Anytime baking trays are referenced in this book, this is the size I am referring to.

✓ 2 x 12-cup muffin pans

 ✓ 1 x 9- x 5-inch (23 x 13 cm) loaf pan

 ✓ 1 x 9-inch (23 cm) round cake pan

✓ 2 x 12-cup (or 1 x 24-cup) mini muffin pans

 ✓ 1 x 10-inch (25 cm) metal tart pan

✓ 2 x madeleine pans

 ✓ 8 x standard ramekins 3½ inches (9 cm) in diameter and
1½ inches (4 cm) high with a capacity of ½ cup (125 mL)

 ✓ 4 x shallow ramekins 5 inches (13 cm) in diameter and 1¼ inches
(3 cm) high with a capacity of ½ cup (125 mL)

 ✓ 6 x heart-shaped porcelain molds with holes in the bottom and
a capacity of ½ cup (125 mL)

BAKING EQUIPMENT

cookie scoop

There are no cookies in this book requiring a scoop but there are recipes
where a scoop comes in handy. Both the Crunchy Fish Cakes (p. 103) and
Crispy Vegetable Cakes (p. 111) are quick and easy to portion with a cookie
scoop, Cheese Puffs (p. 85) and *Profiteroles* (p. 139) can be scooped out
and even some of the tea-cake-type recipes (*Madeleines*, p. 65, or
Financiers, p. 69) are easier to carefully pour into their molds with a
cookie scoop. I recommend a couple of different sizes (1 tablespoon,
1½ tablespoons and 3 tablespoons) to start with. Once you've used them
with the recipes in this book, use them to scoop out cookies. If, like me,
you are a relative newcomer to their use, you'll be wondering why you
waited so long. These are no longer optional in my kitchen, and the boys
love to use them too.

piping bags and tips

There are a few recipes that call for piping, so either invest in a few reusable piping bags (made from fabric and coated in plastic) or purchase disposable bags. Both are widely available at baking supply stores. The largest size you will need for recipes in this book is 18 inches (45 cm). Pair them with a couple of piping tips (¾-inch/2 cm opening): one open star tip (for *Éclairs*, p. 143) and one plain tip (for Traditional Macarons, p. 80, or *Profiteroles*, p. 139).

To fill a piping bag, place the piping tip in the bag, pushing it snugly into the end of the bag. If you're using a disposable bag, cut off the plastic end; if you're using a reusable bag, just make sure the tip is snug in the end of the bag. Twist the tip end so it's closed; this will mean less chance of mixture spilling out when you pick it up. Place the bag, tip side down, in a large, tall glass or jug and make sure the open end is as wide open as it can be. If your glass allows, you can fold the bag over the rim to help it stay open. Scrape the pastry, batter or mixture into the piping bag, then remove the bag from the glass and lay it flat on a worktop. Push the pastry, batter or mixture down to the tip end until it's just about at the open end of the tip (a plastic bench scraper is great for this). Twist the wide end of the bag to seal it closed. Always hold your piping bag tip end up unless you're actually piping!

cookie cutters

The cookie recipes in the book will specify cutters of a certain size. Do your best to use as close to the suggested size as possible, otherwise your baking times will need to be adjusted.

parchment paper

I prefer to use parchment paper over silicone baking mats because it's more consistent. Silicone mats can vary in thickness and quality, meaning that the heat is conducted differently from mat to mat, which might produce inconsistent (and sometimes unsuccessful) results.

a rolling pin (adjustable or with spacers)

I prefer a French, straight rolling pin, which doesn't have handles on the end, as I find it gives the most control. For kids, it encourages them to roll and stretch the dough rather than pressing it into the work surface (which they do when they have a pin with handles). Rolling dough out to an even thickness is not something I am naturally gifted at, so I rely on a rolling pin with plastic rings of varying sizes that fit on each end to help roll the dough to the correct thickness. Joseph Joseph makes an excellent one, but if you don't have this type of pin, you can purchase rubber spacers or rings (elastic bands of varying thicknesses) to slip on the end of your rolling pin. Try one of these methods—it will make rolling cookies so much easier.

POTS AND PANS

It's always good to have a variety of pots and pans. As well as your usual set of pans, I recommend:

✓ 1 x 10-inch (25 cm) nonstick skillet

✓ 1 x 9-inch (23 cm) nonstick skillet

✓ 1 x 10-inch (25 cm) cast-iron skillet with griddle marks

✓ 1 x 3-quart (2.8 L) ovenproof sauté pan (note that these are heavy and hot for children to handle so they need to be used with adult supervision)

✓ 1 x 3½ quart (3.5 L) ovenproof pot like a Dutch oven

OTHER POTS AND PANS

For the recipes in this book, you'll need:

✓ 1 x roasting pan (15 x 10 x 5½ inches/38 x 25 x 14 cm)

✓ 1 x 5- x 7-inch (13 x 18 cm) ovenproof baking dish

✓ 1 x 10- x 12-inch (25 x 30 cm) ovenproof baking dish

✓ 1 x 10- x 7- x 2-inch (25 x 18 x 5 cm) deep ovenproof baking dish

✓ 1 x 2-quart (2 L) casserole dish

MISCELLANEOUS EQUIPMENT

colander

You'll need a colander for many of these recipes. Use it for draining pasta or vegetables, or to wash your vegetables before you prepare them.

wire strainer/sieve

There are a few recipes in the book for mashed potatoes (Shepherd's Pie on p. 89 and the Silky Potato Purée on p. 112). For excellent results, you can use a ricer to get the potatoes super smooth, but you can also use a wire strainer/sieve, which you probably already have in your kitchen. You don't need very fine mesh for this—a medium-sized hole will be fine. You may also need to strain out your *crème pâtissière* (p. 129) and a metal sieve works well here.

CUTTING, CHOPPING AND GRATING

knives

One of my very young cooking club members told his dad after the first session: "She gave kids knives to work with. She's either really cool or really crazy. Or maybe both!" This is perhaps true in part, but my feeling is that kids need to learn proper knife skills from the beginning, before they start to think about it as being "difficult." Many parents wonder about giving their children real knives to work with, but I think it's an important learning experience.

In cooking club and when I'm cooking with my French classes, budget is a factor because I can have up to 23 kids chopping at the same time. The knives we use are small paring knives (we have serrated and non-serrated versions for different tasks). For my own kitchen, I really like the Opinel 112 and 113 paring knives. Paring knives are an excellent entry point into the world of knife skills for children. With a smaller blade, it's easier to teach kids the correct way to use a knife, knowing that you might need to jump in with a larger chef's knife sometimes. To this day, I've only ever used paring knives with the boys at school and we do okay! At home, once they've mastered basic knife skills, I'd recommend graduating them to a 7-inch (18 cm) chef's knife. It's the perfect size for growing hands and gives them more control than a paring knife. Remember that a dull knife is more dangerous than a properly sharpened one as they can slip on whatever you're cutting and potentially cut you, so make sure you keep them sharp. And keep a supply of Band-Aids on hand too!

vegetable peeler

Peeling vegetables is a great job for younger children as long as they have the correct tool. I like the y-shaped (European-style) peelers with a wide blade because they give small hands the most control.

box grater and rasp

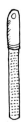

Many of the recipes in the book call for vegetables or cheese to be grated. It might seem boring, but my students fight to use both the box grater and the rasp (Microplane). Seriously, if they come into the lab and spy these tools on the equipment bench, there are always cries of "I've got dibs on the grater!" These tools can be very sharp, so make sure you show children how to use them properly: hold onto the handle at the top, go slowly, keep fingers away from the sharp grate, and you shouldn't have any trouble. The beauty of this is that there are always "ends" of vegetables or cheese that are too small to grate, so if it's edible in its raw state, it can be a chef's treat—trust me, there's nothing like a bit of grating to work up a kid's appetite.

kitchen scissors

You might think you don't need such a thing but scissors are super useful in the kitchen. From cutting parchment paper to fit a baking tray, snipping the top of your Breakfast Rolls (p. 31) to make a pretty shape, snipping herbs (like the basil in the Individual Baked Eggs on p. 39) to simply opening packages, a sturdy pair of kitchen scissors will come in handy.

pizza cutter

I often use my pizza cutter for cutting or trimming pastry. You can buy special tools for this but I like to use what I have on hand.

GADGETS

kitchen timer

Although nowadays we all have timers built into our phones and other devices, I still like to have a separate timer for cooking. It's too easy to accidentally cancel a timer on a device when you are swiping around the screen and, of course, there's the issue of the screen being exposed to all those ingredients. Liquids, flour and butter shouldn't really come into contact with devices (I am speaking from much experience here). Buy a cheap timer and use it only for cooking and baking, perhaps in conjunction with the timers on your stove or microwave, although I have been guilty of accidentally turning those off too. A digital display is the most precise.

oven thermometer

Did you know that the temperature inside your oven might not be the temperature it says it is on the dial/display? It's true! An in-oven thermometer will tell you the true temperature inside the oven, where it counts, so you can adjust the temperature you set accordingly if your oven runs hot or cold.

instant-read thermometer

Also sold as meat and candy thermometers, these will accurately tell you the temperature of your meat, milk or liquid, for when you are heating it to mix with yeast, and even the internal temperature of your breads. It's a relatively inexpensive investment to ensure your meat is correctly cooked or your baking yeast doesn't die from being mixed with over-heated liquid.

kitchen blowtorch

This is not absolutely essential but do know that an inexpensive kitchen blowtorch can transform the sugar on the top of your *Crème brûlée* (p. 134) in a way that an oven broiler simply can't. Kids, closely supervised, absolutely love this tool (because, fire, obviously!). Put one on your wish list.

BREAKFAST
le petit déjeuner

Breakfast in France isn't a huge meal and focuses on baked goods like breads with butter and jam or perhaps a croissant. A child's breakfast might include a yogurt. In this chapter, you'll learn to make some classic breakfast foods—from bread and "quick" croissants (not necessarily quick to make but a faster method than the traditional recipe, so more accessible for young chefs), to a creamy yogurt pot. There's something for everyone who wants to bring a little of France to their morning routine. For those looking for a more substantial dish, I've included two typical French egg dishes—perfect for "*le brunch*!"

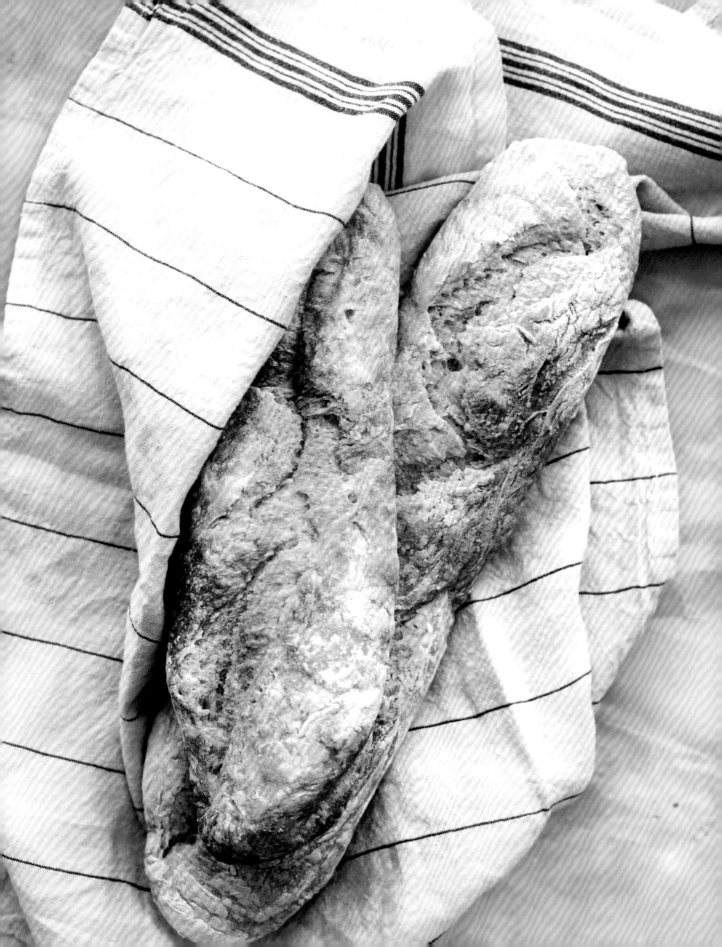

no-knead french loaf
{ pain français facile }

Makes two (12-inch/30 cm) loaves

Prep time (see suggested timetable):
Active time: 1 hour
Resting time (Day 1):
2 to 3 hours
Chilling time: overnight
(or up to 5 days)
Proofing time (Day 2):
1½ to 2 hours

Bake time: 35 minutes

∾

INGREDIENTS

1¾ cups (430 mL) water

3 cups (450 g) all-purpose flour

1½ teaspoons fine sea salt

1½ teaspoons instant yeast

Olive oil, for greasing the bowl

All-purpose flour, for rolling and shaping

SPECIAL EQUIPMENT

Spray bottle (optional)

You could hardly write a French food cookbook without a nod to one of France's best-known foods, the baguette. For most home bakers, the authentic baguette you buy in *boulangeries* in France is difficult to make at home because our ovens simply don't get hot enough to produce the fabulously crispy crust. This recipe is a variation on the "no-knead" technique of bread baking popularized by Jim Lahey (of Sullivan Street Bakery in New York). It makes an excellent French-style loaf that's doable at home with very little hands-on time at all. Note that the dough needs to rest overnight in the fridge but it can stay there for up to 5 days; it's a great recipe to make in advance. I usually prepare one loaf at a time and save the remaining dough for another day.

1. Heat the water to between 110°F and 113°F (approx. 45°C) in a medium pot over medium-high heat (use a digital thermometer to measure the temperature). If heating in a microwave, use a microwave-safe bowl and start with 30 seconds on high. If it's not hot enough, you can continue to heat in increments of 15 seconds, to be sure not to overheat. Pour the water into a large bowl.

2. In a separate bowl, whisk the flour, salt and yeast together, then add them to the water. Use a wooden spoon to stir everything until the dough starts to come together. It will be shaggy, soft and very sticky at this stage.

3. Lightly oil a large bowl (about a 6-cup/1.5 L capacity), scrape the dough into it and then cover the bowl tightly with plastic wrap. I use two layers and make sure they're tightly pulled across the top so that they don't sink down and stick to the dough. Poke a few holes in the plastic wrap and leave the dough to rest at room temperature for 2 to 3 hours.

4. Transfer the bowl to the fridge and refrigerate it overnight (or for up to 5 days).

5. When you are ready to bake, remove the dough from the fridge. Sprinkle a large piece of parchment paper with about 1 tablespoon of flour. Use a plastic bench scraper or a blunt knife to cut the dough in half. It will still be very sticky. Work with one piece of the dough at a

Though it might seem like baguette is the only bread the French eat, there are lots of other loaves available to buy in France. It's good to know their names when you're working with this recipe because depending on what size and shape your bread ends up, you can tell people it's *une ficelle* (a thin, long loaf), *une flûte* (a fatter, shorter loaf) or *une demi baguette* (around 12 inches/30 cm long and 3 inches/8 cm wide).

A suggested timetable:

Day 1: Make the dough (15 minutes' active time), leave it at room temperature for 2 to 3 hours and then refrigerate overnight.

Day 2: Remove the dough from the fridge, roll and shape the baguette(s), proof for 1½ to 2 hours and then bake for 35 minutes.

time to make one loaf. Shape the dough into a rough oval and sprinkle a little flour on top.

6. Lightly flour a rolling pin and roll out the dough to an 8- x 4-inch (20 x 10 cm) oval.

7. Working from the long side, fold the dough in half—you may need a plastic bench scraper or a spatula to help you lift the dough—and gently press the edges together with your fingers.

8. Use the rolling pin (you may need to flour it again) to roll the dough so it is 8 x 4 inches (20 x 10 cm) again and, working from the long side, fold it in half again. Use your fingers to press the edges together to make a seam.

9. Place the seam side of the dough facing down and place your hands around the dough without squeezing it. Gently roll and stretch the dough underneath your hands on the parchment paper, not applying any pressure, so it stretches to about 12 inches (30 cm) long.

10. Carefully lift the parchment paper onto a baking tray, lightly sprinkle the loaf with some flour and cover with a clean, dry tea towel. Let the loaf proof for 1½ to 2 hours. Repeat with the second half of the dough and place it on a separate tray. You can store the second half in an airtight bowl, for up to 5 days in the fridge.

11. With 30 minutes of the proofing time to go, preheat the oven to 450°F (230°C).

12. When the oven is at temperature, remove the tea towel from the loaf and use a very sharp knife at about a 45-degree angle to make three or four diagonal slashes in the top of the loaf. The key to doing this is a sharp knife and a quick, decisive movement. Don't overthink it.

13. Spray the top of the loaf lightly with water in a spray bottle (or use your hand to sprinkle the water over top), then quickly slide the bread tray into the oven.

14. Bake for 35 minutes. The top of the bread should be golden brown and have a nice crust, and the bread should sound slightly hollow if you tap the bottom of it.

15. Allow to cool slightly before you eat it, if you can wait! This is best eaten on the day it's made, though it makes mighty fine toast the next day.

quick croissants
{ croissants }

Makes 10 croissants

Prep time (see suggested
timetable):
Active time: 1¾ hours
(in three stages)
Chilling time: 1 hour,
plus 3 hours to overnight
Proofing time: 3 hours

Bake time: 20 to 25 minutes

∾

INGREDIENTS

½ cup (125 mL) 2% milk

2½ teaspoons active dry yeast

1½ cups (225 g) all-purpose
flour

¼ cup (50 g) granulated sugar

1 cup (226 g) cold salted butter
or European-style butter, cut
into rough cubes

All-purpose flour, for rolling
and shaping

1 egg, lightly beaten

1 tablespoon heavy (35%)
cream

Typically, croissants are made using a laminated dough, where layers of butter are rolled and folded into the layers of dough. This is a complex technique that takes the better part of a day to do properly and doesn't really belong in a book of "easy, everyday" recipes for children, but I couldn't write a French cookbook and not include a recipe for croissants. This one borrows a technique from the great Julia Child, who borrowed it from Beatrice Ojakangas (author of *The Great Scandinavian Baking Book*) for inclusion in *Baking with Julia*. It produces a fluffy, rather than super-flaky, croissant. This is definitely one of the more advanced recipes in the book, not because it's difficult, but because it requires a bit of planning and some precision in the rolling and folding. But if you set out to make this a weekend project and take each step slowly, you'll be thrilled with the results.

1. Heat the milk to between 110°F and 113°F (approx. 45°C) in a medium pot over medium heat (use a digital thermometer to measure the temperature). If heating in a microwave, use a microwave-safe bowl and start with 30 seconds on high. Continue to heat in increments of 15 seconds and be sure not to overheat.

2. Pour the milk into a large heatproof bowl and sprinkle the yeast over it. Let it sit for 10 minutes. It will be slightly frothy on top after this time.

3. Meanwhile, place the flour, sugar and then the butter in the bowl of a food processor fitted with a metal blade. Pulse eight to ten times— you should still be able to see large chunks of butter.

4. Tip the flour/butter mix over the warmed milk and use a wooden spoon to just incorporate the dry ingredients into the milk. The dough will be lumpy, shaggy and quite dry at this point.

5. Use your hands to form a ball of dough. It might need a bit of work, but keep going—it will come together! Cover the bowl tightly with plastic wrap and place it in the fridge for at least 1 hour (don't leave it much longer than this, though, because it will become too difficult to roll out).

6.   Remove the dough from the fridge and lightly flour your countertop. Knead the chilled dough gently until you can feel it becoming softer. Use your hands to shape it into a rough rectangle.

7.   Lightly flour a rolling pin and roll out the dough until you have a very large rectangle (8 x 17 inches/20 x 40 cm). You should be able to see butter pieces in the dough. If the edges of the rectangle crack a little as you are rolling, simply push them together with your fingers and continue to roll until you have the correct size of rectangle.

8.   Fold the top of the dough about two-thirds of the way down, then fold the bottom third up over the first fold. You might need a plastic bench scraper or spatula to help you scoop up the dough if it's sticking a little.

9.   Turn the block of dough clockwise so the seam (the open side) is on your right. This rolling and folding is known as a "turn."

10. If the dough or work surface is sticky, lightly flour the surface, brushing off any excess flour with your fingertips or a pastry brush, and lightly flour the rolling pin again. Repeat Steps 7 through 9 seven times for a total of eight "turns." Make sure you brush the excess flour off the pastry and the rolling pin each time, though you shouldn't need very much extra flour. This dough is very smooth and elastic and rolls beautifully.

11. Wrap the dough tightly in plastic wrap and refrigerate for a minimum of 3 hours, but preferably overnight.

12. Line two baking trays with parchment paper. Remove the dough from the fridge and place a large piece of parchment paper on your countertop or table. Let the chilled dough sit for a few minutes so it's not completely cold when you start working with it. Roll the dough until you have a rectangle that is a little over 8 x 24 inches (20 x 60 cm). This may take a bit of patience, but if you take it slowly, the dough will definitely roll out this large. Trim the edges of the rectangle so they are neat and straight—a tape measure and pizza cutter work well for this.

13. Working along the long sides of the rectangle, make a small cut in the dough on each side of the rectangle every 4½ inches (12 cm). Place a tape measure across the width of the dough at the first mark. Use a long sharp knife or a pizza cutter to cut a rectangle across the width of the dough. Repeat at each mark until you have five rectangles.

These do require a bit of planning but they are so worth the effort! A suggested timetable is as follows:

Day 1: 60 minutes' hands-on time, in stages, 60-minute rest in fridge. Refrigerate overnight.
Day 2: 45 minutes' hands-on time (rolling, measuring), 3 hours' proofing time, 20 to 25 minutes' bake time.

14. Cut each rectangle in two diagonally to make two triangles. Use a tape measure (to make sure the triangles are even) and a pizza cutter to do this. You'll have 10 triangles.

15. Gently stretch one of the triangles at each corner, then, working from the wide end, roll up the dough until you have reached the pointed end. *Voilà*, you have a croissant. Repeat with the remaining triangles. You might find that some of your croissants are not quite the shape you think they should be—again, practice makes perfect and they will still taste amazing!

16. Place five croissants on each tray and cover each tray with a clean tea towel. Leave to rest in a warm place for 3 hours. The croissants will puff up slightly during this time.

17. When the croissants have been resting for 2½ hours, preheat the oven to 375°F (190°C). Whisk the egg and cream together and gently brush the tops of the croissants with this egg wash.

18. Place one tray in the top third of your oven and the other in the bottom third of the oven. Bake for 20 to 25 minutes, or until the croissants are golden brown on top. Switch the trays from top to bottom and turn them from front to back halfway through baking.

19. Remove the baking trays from the oven. Let the croissants sit on the baking trays for about 10 minutes, then place them on a wire rack to cool completely (if you can wait). They will keep for 2 to 3 days in a resealable plastic bag (you can pop them in the microwave to reheat for a few seconds).

Have you ever wondered why even though the word *"croissant"* means "crescent," many croissants are straight, not crescent-shaped? In France, shaping a croissant straight as opposed to rounded is a way of showing that it is made with pure butter (as opposed to margarine or another fat). You'll often see them sold as *croissants au beurre* (butter croissants) and *croissants ordinaires* (ordinary, i.e., NOT butter, croissants). Looking for the croissant's chocolaty cousin the pain au chocolat? You'll find it on page 63 in the After-School Snacks chapter, as it's traditionally enjoyed in the afternoon.

breakfast rolls
{ petits pains au lait }

Makes 12 rolls

Prep time:
Active time: 30 minutes
Proofing time: 1 hour

Bake time: 20 to 25 minutes

∽

INGREDIENTS

1 recipe Simple Brioche Dough
(p. 164)

1 egg, lightly beaten

1 tablespoon heavy (35%)
cream

Pearl sugar, for decorating
(optional)

These are buttery breakfast rolls (sometimes topped with chunky pearl sugar), not unlike brioche, which I discovered at the age of 17, when I was living as an exchange student in Brussels. My host mother would place a basket of fresh *petits pains au lait* on the table, along with some baking chocolate. I still remember the first day I sat at that breakfast table, wide-eyed as I watched my host sisters stuff squares of chocolate inside the little bread rolls. Bread + chocolate for breakfast? Pretty heavenly, right? If you're not as much of a chocoholic as I am, these are also delicious fresh or toasted with butter and jam. Note that this recipe calls for a batch of the Simple Brioche Dough (p. 164) so make sure you take this into account.

1. Follow the simple brioche dough recipe through Step 7. Once your dough has rested for either 1 hour in a warm place or overnight in the fridge, line two baking trays with parchment paper. If your dough was in the fridge, let it sit for about 15 minutes before working with it.

2. Tip the dough out onto a large sheet of parchment paper on a countertop and divide it into 12 equal parts. I cut the dough in halves, then each half into three pieces, which I then cut into two.

3. Take each piece of dough, cup your hand around it and roll it around the parchment to form a smooth ball. Place the dough balls on one baking tray. There will be a seam underneath each dough ball—make sure that stays on the bottom as you place them on the tray.

4. Cover the rolls with a clean tea towel and leave them to rise in a warm place for 30 minutes.

5. Take one of the balls of dough and, using a rolling pin, gently roll it out to a circle about 3 inches (8 cm) in diameter. Flip it over so the smooth side is facing down. Fold the round in half so you have a semi-circle shape. Pinch the edges of the dough together with your fingers and press hard to make sure they stick. Place the dough seam side down back on one of the parchment-lined baking trays and press down gently. You'll have what looks like a long dinner roll with somewhat pointed ends.

6. Repeat with the remaining dough, dividing the rolls evenly between the two baking trays so as not to crowd them.

7. Cover the baking trays with a clean tea towel and leave in a warm place for 30 minutes. Preheat the oven to 375°F (190°C).

8. Whisk the egg and cream together and brush the tops of the rolls with this egg wash. Use kitchen scissors to snip the top surface of the rolls, either in a zig-zag pattern or just three to four diagonal slits on each. Brush the egg wash on again once you have cut the tops and sprinkle the pearl sugar on top if using—approximately 2 teaspoons per roll.

9. Bake for 20 to 25 minutes, or until golden.

10. Remove from the oven and place them on wire racks to cool completely. These are best eaten the day you bake them, but you can also keep them in a resealable plastic bag for up to 3 days (they toast really well!) at room temperature.

creamy yogurt pots
{ petits pots de yaourt à la crème }

Makes six (½-cup/125 mL) ramekins or pots

Prep time: 20 minutes
Chilling time: 4 hours to overnight

∿

INGREDIENTS

1 cup (250 mL) heavy (35%) cream

1 cup (250 g) mascarpone, slightly softened

½ cup (125 mL) 0% plain yogurt

¼ cup (35 g) icing sugar, sifted

½ teaspoon pure vanilla extract

Jam or preserves, for serving

Fresh berries, for serving

SPECIAL EQUIPMENT

Six (½-cup/125 mL) ramekins, small mason jars or yogurt pots

☺ This is a fun dish for kids to assemble. Let them alternate layers of the mascarpone mixture with jam, swirling as they go for a pretty presentation.

When I lived in Europe, I would often enjoy a *fromage blanc* for breakfast. This is a fresh, soft, slightly fermented cheese made from milk and cream. It's a little tangy and pairs beautifully with fresh fruit or compotes for something like fruit-on-the-bottom yogurt, only way better! When I was growing up in Australia, you couldn't buy *fromage blanc* there, but my mum's *Cœur à la crème* (see p. 119) came pretty close in taste. Today you can find *fromage blanc* in some stores outside of Europe, but if you can't, this recipe is a nice alternative to plain old yogurt at breakfast. Served in little mason jars or ramekins with dollops of jam, it makes a perfect special breakfast. Or, you know, an anytime snack . . .

1. In a large bowl, whip the cream with handheld electric beaters on high speed until it forms soft peaks, about 5 minutes. Set aside.
2. In a separate bowl (no need to wash the beaters after you've whipped the cream), beat the mascarpone and yogurt until smooth.
3. Add the icing sugar and vanilla to the mascarpone and continue to beat until smooth and creamy.
4. Using a rubber spatula, gently fold the whipped cream, ⅓ cup (80 mL) at a time, into the mascarpone mixture.
5. Spoon the mixture into ½-cup (125 mL) ramekins or jars, filling each one about three-quarters full.
6. Rap the ramekins or jars on a hard surface to evenly distribute the mixture.
7. Cover each ramekin with plastic wrap. Refrigerate for a minimum of 4 hours or up to overnight.
8. Serve with a spoonful of jam or preserves and some chopped fresh berries.

omelette

Serves 1

Prep time: 10 minutes

Cook time: 5 minutes

∾

INGREDIENTS

2 large eggs

2 tablespoons heavy (35%) cream

Generous pinch of flaky sea salt

Generous pinch of freshly ground black pepper

1 tablespoon unsalted butter

Chives, for garnishing

OPTIONAL FILLINGS

1–2 tablespoons grated cheese (cheddar or Emmenthal work well)

½ small (3 oz/85 g) tomato, diced small and drained on a paper towel

1 slice ham, finely diced

An omelette is a classic French dish that works well for breakfast or lunch. Although the French don't really eat omelettes at breakfast time (it's more a lunchtime dish), *le brunch* is gaining popularity all over France and you'll definitely find omelettes on the menu there. With just a few simple ingredients and endless possibilities for fillings, it's a must-know dish for every child.

1. Whisk the eggs with the cream, salt and pepper in a mixing bowl until just combined. Don't over-whisk.
2. Place a 10-inch (25 cm) nonstick skillet over medium-high heat and melt the butter.
3. Once the butter foam has just about disappeared (don't let it brown), add the eggs.
4. Give the skillet a swirl to distribute the mixture evenly and then let the eggs cook for about 30 seconds.
5. Using a fork, gently stir the eggs in the pan. Swirl the pan to redistribute the uncooked mixture evenly over the surface of the pan. Let it cook for about 30 more seconds.
6. If you're using fillings, add them now—cheese first, then the others, sprinkling evenly over the surface of the omelette.
7. Once the eggs are just barely cooked (or cooked to your liking, if you prefer them more set), either use a flat spatula to flip one side of the omelette over itself to form a half-moon shape or gently roll the omelette up and over the fillings.
8. Slide the omelette onto a plate. Sprinkle with the chives before serving. Serve with flaky sea salt and freshly ground black pepper.

☺ Kids will love making omelettes (with a little supervision for the stovetop part) and personalizing the fillings. Like crêpes (p. 155), these take a little practice to get right, but as long as the eggs are cooked, you can still enjoy them—even if they are a funny shape!

individual baked eggs
{ oeufs en cocotte }

Serves 1

Prep time: 5 minutes

Cook time: 10 to 12 minutes

INGREDIENTS

½ tablespoon unsalted butter, for greasing ramekin

3 cherry tomatoes, cut into quarters

2 tablespoons heavy (35%) cream

1 teaspoon freshly grated cheese of your choosing

1 large egg

1 teaspoon freshly chopped basil

Flaky sea salt, for seasoning

Freshly ground black pepper, for seasoning

Thin slices of bread, for dipping

Like omelettes, this is much more of a weekend or brunch dish as opposed to an everyday breakfast, but I wanted to include it just because I love the name of this dish (so much fun to say!). It's a great, easier alternative to soft-boiled eggs with toast soldiers for breakfast and it's also easy to customize.

1. Preheat the oven to 425°F (220°C).
2. Generously grease a ½-cup (125 mL) ramekin.
3. Place the tomato quarters in the ramekin and pour the cream over them.
4. Sprinkle the cheese on top of the cream and tomatoes.
5. Crack the egg over top, being careful not to break the yolk.
6. Bake for 10 to 12 minutes, or until the egg white is cooked. The yolk will still be runny.
7. Sprinkle the fresh basil over the top of the ramekin, season with salt and pepper and serve with thin slices of bread for dipping.

"Cocotte" is the French word for a baking or casserole dish with a lid. Ironically, oeufs en cocotte are always baked in an open ramekin. But it's still fun to say "cocotte," right?

☺ This is an excellent recipe for beginner cooks. They'll practice greasing ramekins, chopping tomatoes, measuring cream, cracking eggs, chopping basil leaves (they can do this with kitchen scissors too), grating cheese and assembling their dish from start to finish.

LUNCH
le déjeuner

A lot of the dishes in this chapter are inspired by café classics that I like to order when I'm traveling in France. My choices are also based on teaching elementary school–aged children to cook over the better part of a decade and knowing what they like to make and eat. You'll find lots of vegetables here—but don't worry, it's a well-known fact that kids are much more likely to try the foods they prepare themselves, even vegetables. You'll also see a little bit of pastry and lots of cheese (it IS a French cookbook, after all).

creamy vegetable soup
{ velouté de légumes }

Serves 6 to 8

Prep time: 20 minutes

Cook time: 35 minutes

∽

INGREDIENTS

2 tablespoons unsalted butter

1 large (7 oz/200 g) yellow onion, roughly chopped

2 cloves garlic, minced

½ medium (1½ lb/675 g) butternut squash, peeled, seeded and roughly chopped

1 large (7 oz/200 g) carrot, peeled and roughly chopped

3–4 small (7 oz/200 g total) turnips, peeled and roughly chopped

½ medium (7 oz/200 g) cauliflower, roughly chopped

½ teaspoon flaky sea salt

½ teaspoon freshly ground black pepper

2 cups (500 mL) vegetable or chicken stock

2 cups (500 mL) 2% milk

Flaky sea salt and freshly ground black pepper, for seasoning

Sour cream or thick Greek yogurt, for serving (optional)

Though there's nothing particularly French about a vegetable soup, this one reminds me of my time living in Paris when I didn't have a proper kitchen or any space for equipment. I bought a lot of ready-made food through necessity and became slightly addicted to one particular brand of boxed soup whose *Velouté de 9 légumes* I ate nearly every day. A vegetable soup is one of the easiest things you can make, it's a great way to use up leftover vegetables and I've been pleasantly surprised at the eagerness shown by the boys in my cooking club to try vegetables in this form. The creaminess in this recipe comes from using half stock and half milk.

1. Melt the butter in a large pot over medium heat, then add the onion and garlic. Cook for about 5 minutes, stirring occasionally with a wooden spoon until the onion is just starting to soften but not brown.
2. Add the squash, carrots, turnips and cauliflower with the ½ teaspoon salt and ½ teaspoon pepper and give them a good stir in the pot to coat them well with the butter.
3. Pour in the stock and milk, increase the heat to high and bring to a boil.
4. Turn down the heat to a simmer and cook, partially covered (with the lid slightly off the top of the pot), for about 30 minutes. The vegetables should be fairly soft at this point.
5. Remove the pot from the heat and allow the soup to cool slightly.
6. Use an immersion blender or a regular blender to purée the soup.
7. Taste and adjust the seasonings with more salt and pepper, if you like. If you don't find the soup creamy enough, you can swirl in a spoonful of sour cream or thick Greek yogurt just before serving.

The word "*velouté*" means "smooth" or "velvety." It's also the word for a cream soup. Think of how soft velvet is—that's meant to be the texture of the soup once all the vegetables have been blended together.

grilled ham and cheese sandwich
{ croque-monsieur }

Serves 2

Prep time: 15 minutes

Cook time: 15 minutes

INGREDIENTS

FOR THE BÉCHAMEL

1 tablespoon salted butter

1 tablespoon all-purpose flour

½ cup (125 mL) 2% milk

Pinch of flaky sea salt

Freshly ground black pepper

FOR THE SANDWICHES

4 tablespoons unsalted butter, at room temperature

4 slices of day-old white country-style bread

2 slices ham

1 cup (60 g) grated Swiss cheese

"*Croquer*" means to crunch or munch, and refers to the sound you will make when biting into the crunchy toasted bread.

Croque-Monsieur is one of my favorite café meals to eat when I am in France. Traditionally made with square slices of *pain de mie* (white sandwich bread), sandwiched with creamy béchamel sauce, slices of ham and cheese and topped with more béchamel, this is definitely a once-in-a-while indulgence but one that will instantly transport you to a French café.

make the béchamel:

1. Melt the butter in a medium pot over medium-high heat.
2. Once the butter is bubbling, add the flour and cook for 2 minutes, stirring constantly with a wooden spoon, until it forms a paste (called a *roux*).
3. Bring the milk to a simmer in a small pot over medium-low heat, without letting it boil. You can also do this in the microwave in a microwave-safe bowl in 30-second increments until it reaches temperature.
4. Gradually add the warm milk to the flour, stirring constantly. Cook for 3 to 5 minutes, until the mixture thickens slightly, stirring constantly. Remove from the heat and stir in the salt and some pepper.
5. Scrape the béchamel into a clean bowl and allow it to come to room temperature.

make the sandwiches:

1. Preheat the oven broiler to high (400°F/200°C). Heat a nonstick, ovenproof grill pan (preferably a cast-iron skillet with a ribbed base to make "grill" marks) over medium-high heat on the stovetop.
2. Butter each slice of bread on one side only and place two of the slices, butter side down, on the hot griddle pan.
3. Use a spoon to spread about 1 tablespoon of béchamel onto each slice of bread in the griddle pan.
4. Top the béchamel with a slice of ham and one-quarter of the grated cheese.
5. Spread about 1 tablespoon of béchamel onto each of the other slices of bread and place them, butter side up, over the ham and cheese.

Variation: Top your sandwich with a fried egg to make a *Croque-Madame!*

6. Cook for 2 minutes, or until the bottom of the sandwiches are golden.
7. Use a large flat spatula to carefully flip the sandwiches. Gently press the sandwiches down with the spatula.
8. Cook for a further 2 minutes, or until the cheese inside has melted and the bottom of the sandwiches are golden.
9. Remove the pan from the heat and spread 2 tablespoons of béchamel on top of each sandwich. Sprinkle the remaining cheese on the béchamel, making sure to cover the tops of the sandwiches evenly.
10. Transfer to the oven and broil for 3 to 5 minutes, or until the cheese is golden brown and bubbly.

bacon, cheese and onion quiche
{ quiche aux lardons, fromage et oignons }

Makes one (10-inch/25 cm) quiche

Prep time: 30 minutes

Bake time: 45 minutes

∾

INGREDIENTS

FOR THE PASTRY

1 recipe Savory Shortcrust Pastry (p. 166), partially baked (p. 170)

FOR THE FILLING

6 slices bacon

1 small (3½ oz/100 g) yellow onion, diced

½ cup (125 mL) 2% milk

½ cup (125 mL) heavy (35%) cream

3 large eggs, lightly beaten

1 tablespoon smooth Dijon mustard (I prefer Maille)

½ teaspoon flaky sea salt

Freshly ground black pepper, for seasoning

1 cup (60 g) grated Swiss cheese

Once you've mastered shortcrust pastry (p. 166), the world of savory tarts and pies is open to you! This is my favorite basic quiche recipe—you pretty much can't go wrong with bacon, cheese and onion. Note that you need to prepare and partially bake the tart shell before you can begin assembling this dish; you can do this the day before if you prefer.

make the filling:

1. Fry the bacon in a heavy skillet (no need for oil) over medium-high heat until it's just starting to crisp up. You don't want it to cook too much as it will cook again inside the quiche. Remove it from the pan and drain on paper towels. Once it's cool enough to touch, break or chop it into small pieces.

2. Remove all but 1 tablespoon of the bacon fat from the skillet and fry the onion over medium-high heat until it's just translucent. Remove the skillet from the heat and set aside.

3. Whisk the milk, cream, eggs and mustard in a mixing bowl, preferably one with a pouring spout. This will make it easier to pour the custard into the tart shell later. Whisk in the salt and some pepper. Refrigerate until ready to use.

assemble and bake the quiche:

1. Preheat the oven to 400°F (200°C). Line a baking tray with parchment paper.

2. Place the tart pan with the partially baked tart shell on the lined baking tray. Evenly scatter the onion and bacon in the pastry shell. Top with three-quarters of the grated cheese.

3. Gently whisk the egg mixture and pour it over the onions and bacon, shaking the pan a little to evenly distribute the liquid. Scatter the remaining cheese evenly over the quiche.

4. Bake for 45 minutes, or until the filling has set and the middle of the quiche is puffed and golden. Take a peek in the oven about halfway through the bake time. You may need to cover the edges of the pastry shell with aluminum foil so they do not get too brown.

5. Allow to cool slightly before removing from the pan. Serve warm or at room temperature with a green salad.

cheesy pasta bake with ham
{ gratin de pâtes au jambon }

Serves 6

Prep time: 20 minutes

Cook time: 20 minutes

∽

INGREDIENTS

FOR THE PASTA

4 cups (300 g) dry penne pasta

Flaky sea salt, for seasoning

Freshly ground black pepper, for seasoning

FOR THE BÉCHAMEL

¼ cup (57 g) unsalted butter

6 tablespoons (57 g) all-purpose flour

2½ cups (625 mL) 2% milk

FOR THE GRATIN

2 cups (120 g) grated Emmenthal or Swiss cheese

½ teaspoon flaky sea salt

½ teaspoon freshly ground black pepper

6 slices ham, roughly chopped

⅓ cup (28 g) Panko breadcrumbs

This is a French version of mac and cheese, sometimes offered in restaurants as the main course if there happens to be a *menu enfant* (children's menu). Though it's simple, it's a crowd-pleaser for sure. It's quite rich thanks to the béchamel sauce and cheese, so serve small portions of it with a green salad for a pasta lunch with a difference.

prepare the pasta:

1. Cook the pasta according to the directions on the package. Drain and set aside in a large bowl.

make the béchamel:

1. Melt the butter in a medium pot over medium-high heat, being careful not to let it burn.
2. Turn down the heat to medium and add the flour. Cook for 2 minutes, stirring constantly with a wooden spoon. It will be more like a paste than a sauce at this point.
3. In the meantime, in a small pot over medium-low heat, bring the milk to a simmer, without letting it boil. You can also do this in the microwave in a microwave-safe bowl in 30-second increments until it reaches temperature.
4. Gradually add the warm milk to the flour. Cook for 3 to 5 minutes over medium-high heat, until the mixture thickens slightly, whisking constantly. Remove from the heat.

assemble the gratin:

1. Add around one-third of the shredded cheese and the salt and pepper to the béchamel sauce and mix everything well with a wooden spoon.
2. Add the chopped ham to the pasta and mix to distribute evenly. Add the béchamel sauce to the pasta along with half of the remaining grated cheese and stir well to combine the sauce into the pasta.

3. Set the broiler to high (400°F/200°C) and place an oven rack in the middle position. At this point, taste the pasta and adjust the seasoning to your liking with salt and pepper.

4. Spoon the pasta into a large baking dish (roughly 8 x 12 inches/20 x 30 cm) and top with the remaining cheese and the breadcrumbs.

5. Broil for 5 to 7 minutes, or until the cheese has melted and the breadcrumbs are golden.

6. Serve warm with a green salad.

francine's baked stuffed tomatoes
{ les tomates farcies de francine }

Serves 4

Prep time: 25 minutes

Cook time: 40 to 45 minutes

∿

INGREDIENTS

FOR THE TOMATOES

4 large (10 oz/300 g each)
tomatoes

1 small (5 oz/150 g) yellow
onion, finely diced

2 large cloves garlic, minced

½ cup curly parsley, packed
tight, finely chopped

8 oz (250 g) lean ground beef

8 oz (250 g) sausage meat,
casing removed

1 egg, lightly beaten

⅓ cup (28 g) Panko
breadcrumbs

1 teaspoon dried *Herbes de
Provence* or thyme

1 teaspoon flaky sea salt

½ teaspoon freshly ground
black pepper

FOR ASSEMBLY

4 tablespoons Panko
breadcrumbs, plus extra
for garnishing

4 teaspoons olive oil,
for drizzling

When I lived in Belgium as an exchange student, I was introduced to this specialty of one of my host mothers, Francine. I would come home for lunch every day, and this was my favorite meal. A popular version of this dish in the south of France is vegetarian and known as *tomates Provençale* (the filling is breadcrumbs, shallots and herbs), but I like this version with its mix of lean ground beef and sausage meat for added flavor. It's a simple dish with just a few main ingredients, but it looks impressive as you bring it to the table—my favorite kind of dish!

prepare the tomatoes:

1. Preheat the oven to 400°F (200°C). Find a baking dish just big enough to hold all the tomatoes snugly without squashing them, as they can sometimes split and fall apart when they are cooking if the dish is too large.
2. Cut the tops off the tomatoes, around three-quarters of the way up their sides. Keep the "lids" matched with the tomatoes they come from.
3. Use a small, sharp knife to cut around the inside of each tomato and then use a small spoon to scoop out the flesh. Put the flesh and any tomato juices in a separate bowl.
4. Place each tomato upside down to drain on a tray covered with paper towel.
5. Place the onion, garlic and parsley with the beef, sausage meat, egg, breadcrumbs, *Herbes de Provence* or thyme, salt and pepper in a large bowl. Use your hands to mix everything until all the ingredients are thoroughly combined.
6. Prepare your baking dish by pouring in about ¼ cup (60 mL) of the tomato juices from the reserved tomato flesh. You can use the remaining tomato flesh for a pasta sauce, so be sure to refrigerate it.

☺ Many kids are squeamish about touching raw meat, so it's a good idea to have some food-grade plastic gloves on hand (no pun intended). The key to getting the flavor through the meat filling is mixing everything really well and that's a job only your hands can do! For kids who don't want to touch the meat, even with gloves on, there's the less gruesome task of removing the flesh from the inside of the tomatoes—perfect for little hands using a small, sharp knife and a small spoon.

assemble and bake the tomatoes:

1. Place the drained tomatoes right side up in the baking dish. Sprinkle 1 tablespoon of the breadcrumbs in the bottom of each tomato—this will help absorb some of the moisture.

2. Divide the meat mixture into four and place each portion inside a tomato. Replace the lids of the tomatoes and drizzle them with a little olive oil, about 1 teaspoon per tomato. Sprinkle some Panko breadcrumbs on top of each tomato.

3. Bake for 40 to 45 minutes or until the meat filling registers 160°F (71°C) on a digital thermometer.

4. Remove from the oven and allow to cool slightly before removing the tomatoes from the baking dish using a slotted spoon or flat spatula. Serve with a green salad.

creamy celery root salad
{céleri rémoulade}

grated carrot salad
{carottes râpées}

DEJEUNER

couscous salad
{tabbouleh}

trio of salads
{ trois salades }

If you look inside my fridge when I'm in France, there are a few staples that you'll always find. The three salads that follow are part of that group. Though these are supposed to be side dishes, give me a plate with a heaping scoop of each salad, a piece of crusty baguette and some butter and I'll be happy to call it lunch! All these salad recipes make big batches. If you're not going to be eating them immediately, wait to dress them until just before you're ready to serve.

Did you know that the word "*salade*" in French refers to salad greens? If you order *une salade* in a restaurant, they might think you mean *une salade verte*, which is just salad greens (mostly lettuce) and vinaigrette. A *salade composée*, will be a salad with "stuff" in it (hard-boiled eggs, ham, cheese, tomatoes, vegetables and tuna, for example).

grated carrot salad

{ carottes râpées }

Serves 6 to 8

Prep time: 30 minutes

~

INGREDIENTS

FOR THE DRESSING

½ cup (125 mL) vegetable oil

¼ cup (60 mL) fresh lemon juice

2 tablespoons smooth Dijon mustard (I prefer Maille)

½ teaspoon flaky sea salt

¼ teaspoon freshly ground black pepper

1 teaspoon runny honey (optional)

Flaky sea salt, for seasoning

Freshly ground black pepper, for seasoning

FOR THE SALAD

3 large carrots (21 oz/600 g total), peeled and grated

⅓ cup (50 g) golden raisins (optional)

2 tablespoons curly parsley, packed tight, finely chopped

In *My Paris Kitchen*, David Lebovitz says that carrot salad belongs on a list of the top five national dishes of France. He's quite right—it's everywhere. You can find it in *traiteurs* (stores that sell prepared dishes, similar to a delicatessen), in the supermarket and on restaurant menus.

make the dressing:

1. Place the oil, lemon juice, Dijon, salt and pepper in a jar with a tight-fitting lid and shake well. Taste and see how you like it—if you prefer it a little sweeter, you can add the honey. If not, add more salt and pepper, if you like. Refrigerate until you are ready to dress the salad.

make the salad:

1. Squeeze the grated carrots to remove any water, then pat them dry with a paper towel.
2. Place the carrots in a bowl and add the raisins, if using, and the parsley.
3. Dress the salad, using tongs to evenly distribute the dressing. Add a little dressing at a time to see how you like it—you might not need it all.
4. This dish is best served immediately or within a few hours. If you won't be eating this until later, refrigerate and wait to dress until you are just about ready to serve.

☺ Though it's much easier to grate the vegetables in these salads in a food processor, if you are cooking with many children, it's an excellent activity to keep their hands busy (and the texture will be more like the real deal that you get in France). Show them how to hold the vegetables at a 45-degree angle and to turn them around from time to time so they are not grating the same side all the time. If time is tight, or you're making a batch of salad that will last a few days, the food processor is your friend because it's fast and the vegetables will be slightly thicker and less likely to go soggy, which can happen even if they are not dressed.

creamy celery root salad
{ céleri rémoulade }

Serves 6 to 8

Prep time: 30 minutes

~

INGREDIENTS

FOR THE DRESSING

¼ cup (60 mL) mayonnaise

¼ cup (60 mL) 0% plain Greek yogurt

1 tablespoon smooth Dijon mustard (I prefer Maille)

1 tablespoon fresh lemon juice

½ teaspoon flaky sea salt

¼ teaspoon freshly ground black pepper

Flaky sea salt, for seasoning

Freshly ground black pepper, for seasoning

FOR THE SALAD

3 small (2½ lb/1 kg total) celery roots, trimmed and grated

2 tablespoons curly parsley, packed tight, finely chopped

Celery root salad is one I ate for years without really knowing what *céleri-rave* was (I'd never seen it before I moved to France). Nowadays it's much more common and easy to find—look for what my students call "the ugliest vegetable in the store!" This recipe makes a big batch. If you won't be eating it until later, wait to dress it until you are just about ready to serve.

make the dressing:

1. Place the mayonnaise, yogurt, Dijon, lemon juice, salt and pepper in a jar with a tight-fitting lid and shake. Taste and see how you like it. Add more salt and pepper if necessary and refrigerate until you're ready to dress the salad.

make the salad:

1. Squeeze the grated celery root to remove any water, then pat it dry with a paper towel.
2. Place the grated celery root into a separate bowl and add the dressing and parsley, using tongs to evenly distribute them.
3. This is best served immediately or within a few hours.

couscous salad
{ tabbouleh }

Serves 6 to 8

Prep time: 30 minutes

∽

INGREDIENTS

FOR THE DRESSING

⅓ cup (80 mL) olive oil

¼ cup (60 mL) fresh lemon juice

½ teaspoon flaky sea salt

¼ teaspoon freshly ground black pepper

Flaky sea salt, for seasoning

Freshly ground black pepper, for seasoning

FOR THE SALAD

¾ cup (5 oz/150 g) dry couscous

1 small (5 oz/150 g) tomato

1 small (3½ oz/100 g) cucumber

1 small (3½ oz/100 g) orange or yellow bell pepper

¼ cup curly parsley, packed tight, finely chopped

¼ cup chopped fresh mint leaves

Couscous salad is deceptively called *tabbouleh* in French and bears no resemblance to the tabbouleh we're accustomed to in North America, which uses bulgur and herbs. Instead, it's golden grains of couscous studded with colorful vegetables and herbs. This recipe makes a big batch. If you won't be eating this until later, wait to dress the salad until you are just about ready to serve.

make the dressing:

1. Place the oil, lemon juice, salt and pepper in a jar with a tight-fitting lid and shake. Taste and add more salt and pepper if necessary. Refrigerate until you are ready to dress the salad.

make the salad:

1. Cook the couscous according to the directions on the package and allow it to cool. You'll have about 2 cups (500 mL) of cooked couscous.
2. Chop the tomato, cucumber and pepper into small, about ¼-inch (6 mm), cubes.
3. Add the vegetables, parsley and mint to the cooled couscous and mix thoroughly to combine.
4. Add the dressing to the couscous, using a wooden spoon to thoroughly coat the couscous and vegetables.
5. This is best served immediately or within a few hours.

AFTER-SCHOOL SNACKS
le goûter

The school day in France is longer than we are used to in North America, so by the time kids are heading home, they're starving! Enter *le goûter*. Though I've called it an after-school snack, there's no real equivalent for this meal in other countries. The closest I can think of is afternoon tea, since the snacks that are served consist entirely of sweet treats. Because dinner in France is served so late, kids need something to keep them going after their school day, particularly if they have extracurricular activities before they go home. The *goûter* is usually something store-bought that can be eaten on the go, so it might be a cookie or a small cake or even a pain au chocolat. If the *goûter* is eaten at home, it might be simply a piece of bread with a square of chocolate inside (the "real" pain au chocolat!), an open-faced sandwich (called a *tartine*) with jam or chocolate spread, along with a glass of milk or juice. This chapter includes many *goûter* favorites that you can make at home if you don't have the luxury of popping by a *boulangerie* after school!

chouquettes

Makes about 50 puffs

Prep time: 25 minutes

Bake time: 25 minutes

∾

INGREDIENTS

1 recipe Choux Pastry (p. 175)

1 large egg, lightly beaten

1 cup (200 g) pearl sugar

SPECIAL EQUIPMENT

Large (18-inch/45 cm) piping bag fitted with a plain (¾-inch/ 2 cm) piping tip

☺ Choux pastry is an easy recipe for kids to tackle. Kids as young as 7 have successfully made this recipe in my cooking clubs! While piping can be a little challenging, everyone can have a go at forming the shapes using two spoons and younger cooks can help press the pearl sugar into the puffs—it can be time-consuming, so it's a great job for a few kids who see that the more sugar they press into the puff, the more sugar they get to eat.

A traditional after-school snack in France is a bag of *chouquettes*, lovely choux pastry puffs studded with white pearl sugar, usually sold by the 100 g, though if you smile sweetly at the *boulanger/boulangère*, they might throw in a few extra!

1. Preheat the oven to 375°F (190°C). Line two baking trays with parchment paper.
2. Scrape the choux pastry dough into the prepared piping bag and, piping from the top to form a shape not unlike a chocolate kiss, pipe rounds of 1½ inches (4 cm) in diameter, placed about 1½ inches (4 cm) apart. You're looking to form puffs the size of walnuts in their shells. If you don't have a piping bag, you can use a 1-tablespoon cookie scoop or a teaspoon (the kind you stir your tea with, not the measure) to scoop up a heaping spoonful of the mixture, then use a second teaspoon to push it off onto the baking tray, forming a ball as you do so.
3. Dip your finger in water and use it to smooth the tops of each puff, removing any tips that have formed.
4. Brush the tops of the puffs with the beaten egg and gently press the pearl sugar into the dough. You'll need to add a lot more than just a sprinkle as the puffs will expand when they cook, and if you don't add enough, you'll end up with bald *chouquettes*.
5. Place the baking trays in the top and bottom third of the oven and bake for 25 minutes, turning the trays from front to back and switching them from the top to the bottom rack halfway through to ensure even baking.
6. Remove the trays from the oven and transfer the *chouquettes* to a cooling rack. These are best enjoyed the day they are baked, but you can store them at room temperature in airtight containers or resealable plastic bags for a couple of days.

pains au chocolat
{ chocolatines }

Makes 12 pains au chocolat

Prep time (note this does not include the time to make the dough):
Active time: 30 minutes
Proofing time: 3 hours

Bake time: 20 to 25 minutes

INGREDIENTS

1 recipe Quick Croissant dough (p. 27)

24 chocolate baking sticks or ¾ cup (135 g) chocolate chips

1 large egg, beaten

2 tablespoons heavy (35%) cream, for egg wash

SPECIAL INGREDIENTS

The baking sticks used in this recipe are made especially for pains au chocolat. They can be purchased at specialty baking stores, but if you can't find them, chocolate chips will do just fine.

This buttery, chocolaty treat that many people see as a breakfast pastry is actually traditionally enjoyed as an after-school snack. You'll use the same dough as for the Quick Croissants (p. 27) and add some chocolate before you roll them up. Note that these do require a bit of planning. It's a good weekend recipe if you want to bake snacks for the week ahead. This is a two-day project (see suggested timetable) so make sure you plan accordingly.

1. Follow the instructions for making Quick Croissants (p. 27) through Step 11.
2. Line two baking trays with parchment paper. Remove the dough from the fridge and place a large piece of parchment paper (about 24 inches/60 cm long) on your countertop or table. Let the chilled dough sit for a few minutes so it's not completely cold when you start working with it. Cut the dough in half.
3. Roll out one piece of dough until you have a rectangle that is a little over 6 inches (15 cm) wide and 18 inches (48 cm) long. This may take a bit of patience, but if you take it slowly, the dough will definitely roll out to a large rectangle.
4. Trim the edges of the rectangle so they are neat and straight (I use a tape measure and a pizza cutter for this) and measure exactly 6 inches (15 cm) wide and 18 inches (48 cm) long.
5. Working along the long sides of the rectangle, mark every 3 inches (8 cm) with a small cut in the dough on each side of the rectangle.
6. Place a tape measure across the width of the dough at the first mark. Use a long sharp knife or a pizza cutter to cut a rectangle across the width of the dough. Repeat at each mark until you have six rectangles.
7. Place one chocolate baking stick (or sprinkle about ½ tablespoon of chocolate chips) on one of the rectangles across the short end, leaving a border of about ½ inch (1 cm). Tuck the ends of the pastry over the chocolate and begin to roll. Once you have completely covered the chocolate, place a second stick or sprinkle another ½ tablespoon of chocolate chips across the pastry. Continue to roll until you reach the end of the pastry rectangle. Repeat with the other five rectangles.

Suggested timetable:

Day 1 (making the dough):
   60 minutes' hands-on
   time, in stages,
   60-minute rest in fridge.
   Refrigerate overnight.
Day 2: 30 minutes' hands-on
   time (rolling, shaping),
   3 hours' proofing time,
   20 to 25 minutes'
   bake time.

8. Repeat Steps 3 through 7 with the second block of dough.

9. Place six pains au chocolat with the seam side facing down on each tray), and cover each tray with a clean tea towel. Leave to rest in a warm place for 3 hours. They will puff up slightly during this time.

10. When the pains au chocolat have been resting for 2½ hours, preheat the oven to 375°F (190°C). Even if your oven doesn't take that long to preheat, these need a really hot oven, so it's best to preheat for this long. Whisk the egg and cream together to make an egg wash and gently brush the tops of the pains au chocolat with it.

11. Place one tray in the top third of your oven and the other in the bottom third of the oven. Bake for 20 to 25 minutes, or until the pains au chocolat are golden brown on top. Switch the trays from top to bottom and turn them from front to back halfway through baking.

12. Remove the pains au chocolat from the oven, let them sit on the baking trays for about 10 minutes and then place them on a wire rack to cool. These are best enjoyed the same day they are baked, although they will keep for around 3 days in resealable plastic bags. Reheat them in a very cool (250°F/120°C) oven for around 15 minutes or microwave them for 30 seconds.

Did you know that what we call a pain au chocolat is also known as a *chocolatine* in some parts of the south of France?

madeleines

Makes 24 madeleines

Prep time: 15 minutes
Chilling time: 50 minutes
(in 2 stages)

Bake time: 10 to 12 minutes

∽

INGREDIENTS

2 tablespoons (28 g) unsalted
butter, melted, for greasing
the pans

All-purpose flour, for flouring
the pans

½ cup (113 g) unsalted butter

½ cup (100 g) granulated sugar

2 large eggs

1 teaspoon pure vanilla extract

¾ cup (112 g) all-purpose flour

1 teaspoon baking powder

¼ teaspoon fine sea salt

SPECIAL EQUIPMENT

Two 12-cavity madeleine pans

Do you know where *madeleines* get their name? It's said they were originally made in the town of Commercy, in the Lorraine region of eastern France, by a young girl named Madeleine who baked them for the Duke of Lorraine. King Louis XV's wife, Marie, tasted them and brought them back to the royal court where they soon became popular snacks. These small, shell-shaped tea cakes are the perfect *goûter* size—easy to eat on the way home from school and excellent for dipping in hot chocolate. Note that you'll need to prep your pans and chill them at least 30 minutes before you start baking.

1. At least 30 minutes before you start making the madeleines, prepare the pans. Brush the molds with the melted butter, making sure to get the butter into all the grooves. Place a large pinch of flour in each of the molds and shake the pans to coat the butter with the flour. Turn the pans upside down over the sink or over some paper towel to catch the flour, and tap to remove any excess. Put the pans in the freezer for a minimum of 30 minutes while you prepare the batter.

2. Melt the butter either in a small pot on the stovetop over medium heat, or in a microwave-safe bowl in the microwave for about 1 minute. Set aside to cool.

3. Beat the sugar, eggs and vanilla with handheld electric beaters on high speed for 3 minutes, until thick, creamy and slightly pale.

4. In a separate bowl, whisk the flour, baking powder and salt together.

5. Add the dry ingredients to the wet and use a rubber spatula to gently fold them in until the dry ingredients are just combined.

6. Add the cooled, melted butter to the batter and use a rubber spatula to gently mix until the butter is completely incorporated. The batter will be a little runny.

7. Remove one madeleine pan from the freezer and fill each mold about three-quarters full. It's probably easiest to use a small spoon or cookie scoop to fill the molds. There is no need to spread the batter out, it will settle when it bakes. Once you have filled all the molds, place the tray in the fridge.

8. Repeat with the second madeleine pan. Place the pan in the fridge while the oven preheats.

9. Preheat the oven to 400°F (200°C). When the oven is at temperature, remove the madeleine pans from the fridge and then bake for 10 to 12 minutes. Your madeleines should be golden around the edges and may have a bump on top—it can be quite pronounced. Don't worry, that bump is meant to be there!

10. Remove the pans from the oven. Immediately remove the madeleines from the pans to cool on wire racks. They should just pop out of well-greased pans. Madeleines are best the day you make them, but they can be stored in an airtight container at room temperature for a few days. If you glaze them (see below), they are definitely best the day you make them!

option 1: lemon madeleines

1. Rub the zest of a lemon into the sugar (use your fingertips to do this) before you beat it with the eggs for lemon madeleines.

option 2: lemon glaze for madeleines

INGREDIENTS

1 cup (130 g) icing sugar, sifted

¼ cup (60 mL) fresh lemon juice.

1. Whisk the icing sugar and lemon juice together until there are no lumps.

2. Place some parchment paper underneath the wire rack you're using for the madeleines.

3. After the madeleines have cooled for about 10 minutes on the wire rack, dip them in the glaze—first one side, then the other. Let the excess glaze drip off the madeleines and place them back on the wire rack to set.

4. Allow the glaze to harden before you eat them.

Why are these cakes called *financiers*? It's said that they were originally baked in an oval shape by nuns of the Order of the Visitation and called *visitandines*. A clever baker in Paris working near the financial district in the 19th century, one Monsieur Lasne, saw how they could be easily eaten on the go, and thought this would appeal to his busy banker clientele. He shaped the cakes like gold bars and named them *financiers* as a nod to both his clientele and the surrounding district.

financiers

Makes 24 cakes

Prep time: 15 minutes

Bake time: 10 to 12 minutes

∾

INGREDIENTS

Unsalted butter, for greasing
the pan

½ cup (113 g) unsalted butter

4 large egg whites

¾ cup (150 g) granulated sugar

½ cup (50 g) almond meal

⅓ cup (50 g) all-purpose flour

¼ teaspoon fine sea salt

Icing sugar, for sprinkling

Option: Raspberry *financiers*. Just before you bake the *financiers*, cut 12 raspberries in half and place one half, cut side down, on top of each *financier*. Press down gently.

Financiers are another excellent handheld after-school snack. Essentially a tea cake made with a touch of almond meal, these are a little more substantial than *madeleines* (p. 65). They come in various shapes, including rectangles and ovals, and here we're using a mini muffin pan because they're easy to find and many people have them in the kitchen already.

1. Preheat the oven to 400°F (200°C). If you are using a nonstick mini muffin pan you may not need to butter them, but otherwise generously butter the cups of the pan.

2. Melt the butter either in a small pot on the stovetop over medium heat or in a microwave-safe bowl in the microwave for about 1 minute. Set aside to cool.

3. Beat the egg whites until frothy with handheld electric beaters on high speed, 1 to 2 minutes.

4. In a separate bowl, whisk together the sugar, almond meal, flour and salt.

5. Add the dry ingredients to the wet and fold them in gently with a rubber spatula until just combined.

6. Add the cooled, melted butter to the batter and use a rubber spatula to gently mix until the butter is completely incorporated.

7. Divide the batter between the cups of the muffin pan. You can do this with a 1½-tablespoon cookie scoop or a small spoon. Fill each cup almost to the top.

8. Bake for 10 to 12 minutes, or until the center is slightly puffed and the edges are golden and slightly crispy and coming away from the pan. There may be cracks in the tops. That's totally okay!

9. Remove the *financiers* from the muffin pan immediately and allow to cool on wire racks.

10. Once they have cooled completely, sprinkle them with icing sugar to serve. These are best eaten the day they are made, although they can keep for a couple of days in an airtight container at room temperature.

yogurt cake
{ gâteau au yaourt }

Makes one (9-inch/23 cm) round cake

Prep time: 15 minutes

Bake time: 35 to 40 minutes

∿

INGREDIENTS

Unsalted butter, for greasing the pan

All-purpose flour, for the pan

½ cup (100 g) granulated sugar

¼ cup (60 mL) vegetable oil

2 large eggs

2 teaspoons pure vanilla extract

1 cup (250 mL) plain yogurt

1½ cups (225 g) all-purpose flour

2 teaspoons baking powder

Chantilly cream (p. 139) or ice cream and fresh berries, for serving (optional)

This is a simple, not-too-sweet cake that's lovely served with fresh berries. Traditionally, a yogurt cake in France is made using yogurt pots to measure the ingredients. I've adapted the recipe to use standard measures since most of us don't have the classic French yogurt pots on hand.

1. Preheat the oven to 350°F (175°C). Generously butter and flour a 9-inch (23 cm) round cake pan. Place the pan on a sheet of parchment paper, trace around it with a pen, cut it out and use this circle to line the bottom of the pan.

2. Beat the sugar, oil, eggs and vanilla using handheld electric beaters on high speed until light and creamy, about 2 minutes.

3. Fold in the yogurt with a rubber spatula and gently mix until incorporated.

4. In a separate bowl, whisk together the flour and baking powder to combine.

5. Continuing to use the rubber spatula, incorporate the dry ingredients into the wet ingredients and mix until just combined.

6. Scrape the batter into the prepared cake pan, making sure to distribute it evenly. Smooth the top with the back of a spoon or an offset spatula and bake for 35 to 40 minutes, until golden brown on top and springy to the touch. A toothpick inserted in the center of the cake will come out clean when the cake is ready.

7. Remove the cake pan from the oven, place it on a wire rack and allow the cake to cool for 5 minutes.

8. Run a blunt knife between the cake and the pan, place a plate upside down on top of the pan and then, while holding both the plate and the bottom of the pan with oven mitts, carefully flip the cake. This task is best done by a grown-up. Place the wire rack on the cake (this will be the bottom of the cake) and your hand underneath the plate. Flip so it's right side up again. Cool on the wire rack until it comes to room temperature.

9. Serve with a dollop of Chantilly cream or ice cream and fresh berries. Or just eat it on its own.

10. You can store this cake in an airtight container or tightly wrapped in plastic wrap at room temperature for 3 days, though I bet it won't last that long!

Did you know that just as there are different ways to spell "yog(h)urt" in English, depending on where you are from, there are two ways to say it in French: *yoghourt* (yo-GOORT) and *yaourt* (ya-OORT).

french pound cake
{ quatre-quarts }

Makes one (9- x 5-inch/23 x 13 cm) loaf

Prep time: 15 minutes

Bake time: 45 to 55 minutes

∽

INGREDIENTS

Salted butter, for greasing the pan

All-purpose flour, for the pan

1 cup (226 g) salted butter

4 large eggs

1 cup (200 g) granulated sugar

1½ cups (225 g) all-purpose flour

2 teaspoons baking powder

Vanilla ice cream or Chantilly cream (p. 139) and fresh berries for serving (optional)

The name of this cake in French translates to "four fourths," because all four main ingredients (butter, eggs, sugar and flour) are used in equal parts. For this reason, the conversions to cups is a bit awkward, so I've rounded both the weight and the equivalent volume up or down to make things a little easier.

1. Preheat the oven to 350°F (175°C). Generously butter and flour a 9- x 5-inch (23 x 13 cm) loaf pan. Place the pan on a sheet of parchment paper, trace around it with a pen, cut it out and use this parchment to line the bottom of the pan.
2. Melt the butter in a small pot over low heat or in the microwave in a glass bowl. Set it aside to cool slightly.
3. Beat the eggs and sugar with handheld electric beaters on high speed until thick, pale and light in color, 2 to 3 minutes.
4. In a separate bowl, whisk together the flour and baking powder to combine.
5. Using a rubber spatula, mix the dry ingredients into the wet ingredients until just incorporated.
6. Gently pour in the melted, cooled butter and mix with a rubber spatula until completely combined.
7. Pour the batter into the prepared loaf pan and bake for 45 to 55 minutes, until golden brown on top and springy to the touch. A toothpick inserted into the center of the cake will come out clean.
8. Remove the cake pan from the oven, place it on a wire rack and allow the cake to cool for 10 minutes in the pan.
9. Run a blunt knife between the cake and the pan to loosen it, then unmold it, allowing it to come to room temperature on the wire rack, right side up.
10. Serve with ice cream or Chantilly cream and fresh berries. Or just eat it on its own.
11. You can store this in an airtight container or well covered with plastic wrap at room temperature for 2 to 3 days. Beyond that, it might be a little dry, but if you slice it thickly you can toast it—it's really good with butter and jam for breakfast!

mini jam tarts
{ tartelettes à la confiture }

Makes 20 tartlets

Prep time:
Active time: 30 minutes
Chilling time: 30 minutes

Bake time: 20 minutes

∽

INGREDIENTS

1 recipe Sweet Shortcrust
Pastry (p. 168)

All-purpose flour, for rolling
dough

Unsalted butter, for greasing
the pans

About ½ cup (125 mL) jam,
any flavor

SPECIAL EQUIPMENT

Rolling pin with spacers to
ensure the dough is the correct
thickness (see p. 17)

I do love a good jam tart, and these are an attempt to recreate a store-bought version that I couldn't get enough of when I lived in Paris. Though they are a simple recipe, they are impressive to look at and make a pretty presentation, especially if you use different flavors (and colors) of jam. Note that you can make the pastry the day before.

1. Follow the sweet shortcrust pastry recipe through Step 4.
2. Remove the disk of dough from the fridge and let it sit for a few minutes so it's easier to work with. Cut the dough in half.
3. Lightly flour a large sheet of parchment, then place one piece of dough on the parchment. Sprinkle it lightly with flour and place a second sheet of parchment paper on top.
4. Roll the dough between the two sheets of parchment paper to a thickness of ⅙ inch (4 mm). If the dough is soft, you might need to put it back in the fridge to firm up a little before you cut it.
5. Preheat the oven to 375°F (190°C). Lightly grease two 12-cup muffin pans with butter.
6. Using a cookie cutter that's about 3 inches (8 cm) in diameter, cut out rounds of the dough. A cookie cutter with fluted edges makes for pretty tartlets but if you don't have a cookie cutter, you can use a glass or ramekin that's the same diameter. One disk of the pastry should make ten rounds. You will need to gather up and re-roll scraps of the pastry to make sure you get ten—and each time you re-roll, you will need a touch of flour to ensure the pastry does not stick to the parchment. You may need to refrigerate the dough again once it's been rolled out if it is very soft and sticky.
7. Use an offset spatula to help you remove the pastry rounds from the parchment and gently place them in the muffin cups. You don't need to press them right down to the bottom, as gravity will help them sink to form a little cup. Make sure the pastry rounds are evenly centered in the muffin cups. Place the muffin pan in the fridge while you work with the second piece of dough.
8. Repeat with the second piece of dough and refrigerate the muffin pan and pastry rounds for 30 minutes.

Depending on the type of jam you use (and its sugar vs fruit content), it may not spread as it cooks. If your jam doesn't spread, add another teaspoon of the jam when the tartlets are just out of the oven and gently swirl to combine the hot and cold jams. Allow to set as per the recipe.

9.   Place 1 teaspoon of jam in the middle of each pastry round. It doesn't look like a lot but it will bubble up and expand when it cooks.

10.   Bake for 20 minutes, until the pastry is golden and the jam is bubbling.

11.   Remove the pans from the oven and let the tarts sit in the pans for about 15 minutes, or until the jam is no longer runny. Remove the tartlets from the pans and cool on wire racks. Serve at room temperature. You can store these in an airtight container for up to 3 days—they will get soggy the longer you store them, though, so best to eat them up!

palmier cookies
{ palmiers }

Makes about 20 cookies

Prep time:
Active time: 15 minutes
Chilling time: 30 minutes

Bake time: 15 to 17 minutes

∾

INGREDIENTS

1 sheet store-bought puff pastry (8 oz/250 g), thawed but chilled, or ½ recipe of Rough Puff Pastry (p. 171) rolled out to 10 x 10 inches (25 x 25 cm), chilled

1 tablespoon water

¼ cup (50 g) granulated sugar

Granulated sugar, for baking

With just two main ingredients—puff pastry and sugar—these cookies couldn't be easier, especially if you happen to have a roll of puff pastry on hand. They are the perfect teatime treat, especially when paired with a mug of hot chocolate. Note that you can use homemade rough puff pastry (p. 171) or store-bought for this recipe. If you make your own pastry, you can make it the day before and use it straight from the fridge.

1. Line a baking tray with parchment paper and set aside. Place a piece of parchment paper about 10 x 10 inches (25 x 25 cm) on a work surface.

2. If using store-bought pastry, make sure it is 10 x 10 inches (25 x 25 cm). If using homemade puff pastry, roll it out to 10 x 10 inches (25 x 25 cm) on parchment paper. Use a pastry brush to lightly brush the water over the surface of the pastry.

3. Sprinkle half of the sugar evenly over the surface of the pastry. Use a rolling pin to lightly press the sugar into the dough.

4. Fold the left and right sides of the pastry inwards so they meet in the center. Sprinkle the remainder of the sugar over the pastry and use the rolling pin to lightly press this sugar into the dough.

5. Fold the left and right side of the pastry inwards again, so they meet in the center again, and then fold the pastry in half lengthwise.

6. Wrap this pastry log tightly in plastic wrap and refrigerate for 30 minutes.

7. Preheat the oven to 400°F (200°C).

8. Remove the pastry log from the fridge and place it on a cutting board.

9. Using a very sharp knife, cut the log into about 20 slices, each one ½ inch (1 cm) wide. Lay the slices flat on the baking tray about 2 inches (5 cm) apart. Sprinkle a pinch of sugar on each cookie.

10. Bake the cookies for 10 minutes, then flip them over and bake for a further 5 to 7 minutes, until they are golden and crispy. Keep an eye on them in the final minutes of baking as they can go from perfect to scorched in a matter of seconds.

butter cookies
{ petits-beurre }

Makes about 30 cookies

Prep time:
Active time: 45 minutes
Chilling time: 1 to 3 hours

Bake time: 11 to 13 minutes

∽

INGREDIENTS

1½ cups (225 g) all-purpose
flour

½ cup (100 g) granulated sugar

1 teaspoon baking powder

½ teaspoon fine sea salt

½ cup (113 g) cold salted
butter, cut into small cubes

¼ cup (60 mL) heavy (35%)
cream

SPECIAL EQUIPMENT

Rolling pin with spacers to
ensure the dough is the correct
thickness (see p. 17)

If you've traveled in France, you might be familiar with the ubiquitous *Petit-beurre* cookie. It has been around since 1886, when it was invented by Louis-Lefèvre Utile in Nantes. The cookies are still imprinted with his initials (LU) and are the best-known product of all the Lefèvre Utile range. This recipe is the closest I can get to my store-bought favorites.

1. Place the flour, sugar, baking powder and salt in the bowl of a food processor fitted with a metal blade. Pulse a few times to combine.
2. Add the cubed butter and pulse until it resembles fine breadcrumbs.
3. Add the cream and continue to pulse until the dough comes together. The dough will be fairly soft.
4. Gather the dough into a ball, divide it in half and form each half into a disk. If you don't want to use it immediately, you can wrap it tightly in plastic wrap and keep it in the fridge for up to 3 days. Roll each disk between two sheets of parchment paper until it's ¼ inch (6 mm) thick. Keeping the dough flat and between the two sheets of parchment, place it in the fridge for 1 to 3 hours.
5. Preheat the oven to 350°F (175°C). Line two large baking trays with parchment paper. Remove one of the rolled-out pieces of dough from the fridge and allow it to sit at room temperature for about 10 minutes.
6. Cut out cookies using a rectangular cookie cutter that measures 2½ x 2 inches (6 x 5 cm). Place the cookies on the parchment-lined baking trays. They will not spread so you can place them fairly close together—just make sure they are not touching.
7. Repeat with the second sheet of dough.
8. Place one tray in the top third of the oven and the other in the bottom third of the oven and bake for 11 to 13 minutes, switching the trays from the top to bottom rack and turning them from front to back halfway through the bake, until the cookies are golden around the edges but still pale in the center.
9. Remove the cookies from the oven and, using an offset spatula, immediately place them on wire racks and allow to cool completely. You can store these in an airtight container for up to 2 weeks.

You can order special *petits-beurre* cookie cutters online if you want the imprint. A true *petit-beurre* has 14 "teeth" on its long side and 10 on the short side and four "ears" in the corners (which are traditionally bitten off first!). But any rectangular cutter that's around 2½ × 2 inches (6 × 5 cm) will do!

traditional macarons
{ macarons à l'ancienne }

Makes about 30 macarons

Prep time: 10 minutes

Bake time: 20 minutes

∾

INGREDIENTS

1½ cups (150 g) almond meal

¾ cup (150 g) granulated sugar

3 large egg whites

Food coloring (optional)

Icing sugar, for dusting

Melted chocolate, for dipping
or drizzling (optional)

SPECIAL EQUIPMENT

Large (18-inch/45 cm)
piping bag fitted with a plain
(¾-inch/2 cm) piping tip

If you've followed my blog or social media over the years, you might have expected a macaron recipe in this book. Well, here it is, but it may not be what you expected (hint: it's even better, because anyone can make them!). Did you know that macarons weren't always those difficult-to-make brightly colored sandwich cookies that we're so familiar with today? The original was a simple cookie made from ground almonds, sugar and egg whites and infinitely more doable than the version you might have already tasted. Macarons that anyone can make? Now that's a concept I can get behind!

1. Preheat the oven to 300°F (150°C). Line two baking trays with parchment paper.
2. In a medium bowl, whisk together the almond meal and sugar.
3. In a separate metal bowl, use handheld electric beaters on medium speed to whip the egg whites to soft peaks, 2 to 3 minutes.
4. Add the dry ingredients to the egg whites, mixing thoroughly with a wooden spoon or rubber spatula. The mixture will be fairly stiff. At this stage, feel free to color the mixture. If you'd like multiple colors of cookie from the same batch, divide your batter before piping them out, color them in separate bowls, then scrape the batter into separate piping bags (you'll need as many bags and tips as you have colors).
5. Transfer the mixture to the prepared piping bag, and pipe out circles of the mixture, about 1½ inches (4 cm) in diameter. There may be a small point on top of each cookie. Simply wet the tip of your finger with a little water and smooth down any points.
6. Using a fine-mesh sieve, dust the tops of the cookies with icing sugar.
7. Place one tray in the top third of the oven and the other in the bottom third. Bake for 20 minutes, switching the trays from the top to bottom rack and turning them from front to back halfway through the bake, until the cookies are just starting to turn golden around the edges. The cookies may crack on top and they will still be a little soft when you remove them from the oven.

8. Remove the cookies from the baking trays with an offset spatula and let them cool completely on a wire rack.

9. Dip these in melted chocolate or drizzle melted chocolate on top, if you like. Or you can simply sprinkle them with more icing sugar. You can store these in an airtight container for up to 1 week.

The history of *macarons* is a complicated one. It's said they originated back in the late 1700s when Carmelite nuns baked cookies with almond meal as a way of supplementing their meat-free diet. During the French Revolution, two nuns in the French town of Nancy started making and selling macarons, and became known as Les Sœurs Macarons. Their original store (La Maison des Sœurs Macarons) still sells macarons today. However, various regions all over France stake their claim to the original macarons. Another version of the story comes from the box of my favorite brand, Bernard Meysan in Saint-Émilion, in southwest France. The box claims Ursuline nuns who settled in Saint-Émilion in 1680 were responsible for the macarons' creation and that one of the sisters shared the secret to making them with some families in the town during the revolution.

DINNER
le dîner

A French home-cooked dinner is a simple affair. In this chapter, you'll find easy recipes, many of which are perfect for weeknight dinners. You'll learn some basic techniques that will hopefully set you on the road to home cooking, French-style. I mean, who doesn't want to learn how to roast a chicken, make excellent oven-baked fries or a rich beef stew? There are also several vegetable and side dishes (ratatouille, three ways!) to choose from, including iconic French potato purée. These simple dishes prepared with fresh ingredients will bring a little bit of France to your dinner table.

cheese puffs
{ gougères }

Makes about 50 puffs

Prep time: 25 minutes

Bake time: 25 minutes

~

INGREDIENTS

1 recipe Choux Pastry (p. 175)

1 cup (60 g) grated Gruyère
or sharp cheddar cheese

You can also freeze these cheese puffs for up to a month once you have scooped them out onto the baking trays (you can place them very close to each other if you are freezing them). Place the trays directly in the freezer and, once they are frozen solid, place the puffs in resealable plastic bags or airtight containers. You can cook them straight from frozen as per the recipe directions, although they may require a few more minutes.

These are likely not the cheese puffs you are thinking of! You may be familiar with choux pastry as the base for sweet treats like *Chouquettes* (p. 61), *Profiteroles* (p. 139), *Éclairs* (p. 143) or even a fabulous Choux Puff Tower (p. 159), but did you know that it makes wonderful savory snacks too? These light and airy puffs have grated cheese added to the mixture at the last minute and are typically served with an apéritif.

1. Preheat the oven to 400°F (200°C). Line two baking trays with parchment paper.
2. Prepare the choux pastry (p. 175).
3. Add the cheese to the pastry and mix with a rubber spatula until just folded through. The dough will be quite thick and sticky.
4. Use a teaspoon (the kind you stir your tea with, not the measure) to scoop a heaping spoonful of the mixture, then use a second teaspoon to push it off onto the baking tray, forming a ball as you do so. You can also use a 1-tablespoon cookie scoop for this job. Don't worry too much about making the puffs perfectly round, as these are meant to be rustic! Leave about 1½ inches (4 cm) between each puff.
5. Bake for 25 minutes with one tray on a rack in the top third of the oven and the other in the bottom third of the oven, turning the trays from front to back and switching them from top to bottom racks halfway through the bake.
6. Remove the trays from the oven and transfer the puffs to a wire rack. Serve warm or at room temperature. These are best enjoyed the day they are made.

☺ Between mixing the eggs into the dough to spooning the puffs out on trays, kids will definitely be kept busy with this recipe. You might see recipes calling for these to be piped out but I actually prefer the look of them when they are spooned out—and that also makes them so much more doable for little (and not so little!) hands.

steak with oven-baked fries
{ steak frites }

Serves 4

Prep time: 20 minutes (steak), 20 minutes plus 1 hour soaking time (potatoes)

Cook time: 60 to 75 minutes

∽

INGREDIENTS

FOR THE FRIES

2 lb (900 g) Yukon Gold potatoes

3 tablespoons olive oil

2 teaspoons flaky sea salt

1 teaspoon chili powder (optional)

¼ teaspoon freshly ground black pepper

FOR THE STEAK

4 boneless ribeye steaks (7 oz/200 g each, around 1 inch/2.5 cm thick)

1 teaspoon flaky sea salt

½ teaspoon freshly ground black pepper

1 tablespoon vegetable oil

TO SERVE

Flaky sea salt

Freshly ground black pepper

Dijon mustard (I prefer Maille)

Mayonnaise and/or ketchup

Steak frites, though a French classic, might seem like more of an adult meal, but in a country where the concept of a children's menu isn't as common as it is in North America, for example, this might be offered as the *plat du jour* for younger diners. It's not unusual to see children eating their steak *saignant* (rare) either, but in this recipe, we cook the steak to medium. The best fries come from a deep fryer, but as that is not a common appliance in most households, I'm opting for oven-baked fries, which are not only less messy, but also easier for kids to cook.

make the fries:

1. Slice the potatoes lengthwise (there's no need to peel them but do scrub them well) into about ½-inch-wide (1 cm) sticks. Don't worry if some of them are shorter than others. The most important thing is that they are more or less the same width.
2. Place the potato sticks in a large bowl of cold water for 1 hour, making sure the water completely covers the potatoes. This will remove the starch, prevent them from sticking together and help them crisp up nicely in the oven.
3. Preheat the oven to 400°F (200°C). Line two baking trays with parchment paper.
4. Drain the potato sticks in a large colander. Place a few sheets of paper towel on a countertop and lay the potato sticks in a single layer. Cover with a few more sheets of paper towel and gently pat them dry. It's important to dry the potatoes as much as you can, otherwise they won't crisp up when you bake them.
5. Place the potato sticks in a large bowl and pour the oil over them, then sprinkle the salt, chili powder (if using) and pepper over top. Using your hands, mix everything well to make sure the potatoes are evenly coated with the oil and spices.
6. Lay the potato sticks in a single layer on each baking tray. Place one tray on the top rack of the oven and the other on the bottom rack.

☺ This might seem like a lot of potatoes to slice up into such precisely sized sticks, but it's a great activity for kids. Tell them why it's important to slice the sticks consistently, and talk them through the process of soaking them to remove the starch. I find that if kids know why they are doing something, it's more meaningful and they're more likely to follow the instructions. Cooking is all about actions and consequences. Maybe they don't slice the sticks very evenly—leave it be, unless the differences are really marked, and show them once they are cooked how some of the fries are too crispy and some aren't done enough. Got younger budding chefs? Drying the potato sticks post-soak on paper towels, patting them dry with more paper towels and coating them with the oil and spice mix in a large bowl is a good way to involve younger children who might not be quite ready to work with knives.

7. Bake for 1 hour, switching the trays from the top to the bottom of the oven and rotating them 180 degrees halfway through, as well as flipping the potatoes with a flat spatula so they crisp up and cook evenly.

8. After an hour, the frites should be crispy and golden. If not, leave them in the oven for 5 minutes at a time, checking often, until they are done.

while the potatoes are baking, prepare the steak:

1. Rub the steaks all over with the salt and pepper. Place them on a plate, cover with plastic wrap and refrigerate until about 20 minutes before you are going to use them, so about 40 minutes into cooking the potatoes.

2. You can pan-sear, broil or grill your steaks. Here we're going to pan-sear them, so you'll need to heat the pan just before you're ready to use it. Place a grill pan (preferably a cast-iron skillet with a ribbed base to make "grill" marks) over medium-high heat and add the oil.

3. Once the oil is hot enough, add your steaks—you should hear an audible "sssssss" when you add the meat if the pan is hot enough—and cook for 3 minutes on each side. The internal temperature as measured with a meat thermometer will be 155°F (68°C) when you take it off the heat and 160°F (71°C) after it has rested.

4. Remove the steaks from the grill pan and place them on a (preferably pre-warmed) plate and loosely cover with aluminum foil. Allow to rest for 10 minutes.

5. Serve the steak with mustard on the side and the fries with ketchup and mayonnaise on the side. (The fries shouldn't need any more salt or pepper.)

shepherd's pie
{ hachis parmentier }

Serves 4 to 6

Prep time: 40 minutes

Cook time: 50 to 55 minutes

∾

INGREDIENTS

FOR THE BEEF FILLING

2 tablespoons olive oil

1 large (7 oz/200 g) yellow onion, finely diced

2 cloves garlic, minced

1 lb (454 g) ground beef

1 cup (250 mL) beef stock

1½ tablespoons tomato paste

1 teaspoon dried *Herbes de Provence* or dried thyme

½ teaspoon flaky sea salt

Freshly ground black pepper

FOR THE MASHED POTATO TOPPING

2 lb (900 g) Yukon Gold potatoes, peeled and chopped

¼ cup (60 mL) heavy cream

2 tablespoons unsalted butter

½ teaspoon flaky sea salt

FOR THE ASSEMBLY

1 cup (60 g) grated Emmenthal or Swiss cheese

Hachis (the "h" and the "s" are silent) *Parmentier* is a classic French dish usually made from leftover beef stew and topped with creamy mashed potatoes. Here we're using ground beef, so you don't need to wait until you have some leftover stew to make this dish.

make the filling:

1. Heat the oil over medium-high heat in a large, heavy skillet. Add the onion and garlic and cook for about 5 minutes, until the onion is just starting to soften but not brown.
2. Add the ground beef and use a wooden spoon to break the meat up (it will help it cook faster). Cook for 8 minutes, until the beef is just starting to brown.
3. Add the beef stock, tomato paste, *Herbes de Provence* or thyme, salt and some pepper, and stir to combine well.
4. Turn down the heat to medium and cover the pan. Simmer for 20 to 25 minutes. Remove from the heat.

make the mashed potato topping:

1. While the beef is simmering, place the potatoes in a large pot of cold water (just enough to cover the potato pieces) over high heat. Bring to a boil and then cook for a further 8 to 10 minutes, or until the potatoes are fork-tender. This will take about 25 minutes in total. Drain the potatoes into a colander.
2. Place a metal sieve over the pot and, using a wooden spoon, press the potato pieces through the sieve (or use a ricer if you have one) to remove any lumps from the potatoes. If you're using a sieve, use a butter knife to scrape the potatoes off the bottom of the sieve as you work. Do not place the pot on the heat again.
3. Add the cream, butter and salt and use a wooden spoon or a rubber spatula to mix everything together until smooth and creamy.

There's some debate about whether the meat filling should include vegetables (diced carrots and turnips, or peas, for example). Here I've kept it simple, but feel free to add vegetables if you like; roughly ½ to ¾ cup diced vegetables or peas would work.

Because the potatoes are going to be cooked and mashed, the size of the pieces doesn't matter so much. Roughly chopping the potatoes is a perfect job for small hands. Pushing the potatoes through the sieve is also a fun job and assembling the dish is doable even for the youngest chefs.

assemble the dish:

1. Preheat the oven to 400°F (200°C).
2. Place the meat filling in a deep casserole dish, about 2 L, making sure to distribute the mixture evenly.
3. Spoon the potatoes on top of the meat filling. Use a rubber spatula to smooth the potatoes right to the edges of the casserole dish. Sprinkle the cheese evenly on top of the potatoes.
4. Bake for 30 minutes, or until the potatoes are crispy and golden and the filling is bubbling away (you might see some of the filling peeking out from under the potatoes). Keep an eye on the dish and check in after around 20 minutes in case it's browning too quickly. If after 30 minutes your potatoes are not crispy and golden, you can set the broiler to high and broil them for 5 to 7 minutes (again, keeping an eye on things!).
5. Allow the dish to sit for a few minutes before serving.

Did you know that the term "*parmentier*" refers to any dish prepared with potatoes? It's a reference to the botanist Antoine-Augustin Parmentier (1737–1813), who spent his life promoting the humble potato, previously seen as only fit to feed to animals, by publishing information about how to grow it and ways to prepare it.

beef and carrot stew
{ bœuf aux carottes }

Serves 4 to 6

Prep time: 25 minutes

Cook time: 45 minutes

∽

INGREDIENTS

1 cup (150 g) all-purpose flour

1 teaspoon flaky sea salt

½ teaspoon freshly ground
black pepper

1½ lb (675 g) stewing beef, cut
into 1-inch (2.5 cm) cubes

2–3 tablespoons vegetable oil

2 cups (500 mL) beef stock

6 slices bacon, diced

2 cloves garlic, minced

6–8 small (7 oz/200 g total)
shallots, roughly chopped

1 large (7 oz/200 g total)
carrot, peeled and diced small

2 teaspoons fresh thyme (or
½ teaspoon dried thyme)

½ teaspoon flaky sea salt

¼ teaspoon freshly ground
black pepper

2 tablespoons tomato paste

FOR COOKING

½ cup (125 mL) beef stock,
for topping up the pot

You might have been expecting a classic *bœuf bourguignon* in a French cookbook but this beef stew is much more appropriate for kids to make and eat. The real thing takes a long time to cook from start to finish, but this is ready in just over an hour, making it doable even for weeknights. And it's even better the next day!

1. Preheat the oven to 350°F (175°C).

2. Mix the flour with the salt and pepper in a large, shallow dish. Roll the cubes of beef, a few at a time, in the flour mixture, shaking them well to remove any excess flour. Place the floured beef on a large plate and continue until all the beef cubes are coated. Discard any remaining flour mix.

3. Heat about 1 tablespoon of the vegetable oil in a large ovenproof pot (around a 3-quart/2.8 L capacity) over medium-high heat. Fry the beef cubes in batches, keeping them in a single layer in the pot, until they are nicely browned on all sides. Remove the browned beef from the pot, place it on a plate and cover with aluminum foil. Continue until all the beef has been browned. You may need to add a little more oil as you work through batches of the beef.

4. Keep the pan on medium-high heat and add about ¼ cup (60 mL) of the stock. Use a wooden spoon to scrape up any brown bits left on the bottom of the pan. The liquid should evaporate completely before you continue. This is known as deglazing the pan. Do not discard the brown bits—they'll add a lot of flavor to the dish.

5. Add the bacon to the pan and fry for 2 to 3 minutes.

6. Add the garlic and shallots and fry for 3 minutes, until the garlic starts to become fragrant and the shallots start to soften.

7. Add the carrots and stir to coat them well with the bacon and shallot mixture. Sprinkle in the thyme, salt and pepper.

8. Pour the rest of the stock into the pot and bring to a boil.

9. Once the stock is boiling, add the beef and the tomato paste. Stir to combine.

10. Place the pot in the oven and cook for 45 minutes, uncovered. Keep an eye on it, though—if it looks like the stock is evaporating too much for your liking, add a splash of the extra stock and stir to combine.
11. Serve with buttered egg noodles or French bread.

It's important in this recipe to have both the beef and the carrots cut in evenly sized pieces. These are both great jobs for younger chefs, though some kids might prefer to wear plastic gloves if they are working with raw meat. Make sure everyone washes their hands thoroughly after working with or touching raw meat too.

pork chops with apples
{ côtelettes de porc aux pommes }

Serves 2

Prep time: 15 minutes

Cook time: 35 minutes

∾

INGREDIENTS

2–3 tablespoons olive oil

2 large (7 oz/200 g each)
bone-in pork chops

2 medium (14 oz/400 g total)
red-skinned sweet apples
(like Gala), skin on, cored
and thinly sliced

1 large (7 oz/200 g) yellow
onion, thinly sliced

¼ cup (60 mL) chicken broth

¼ cup (60 mL) heavy (35%)
cream

½ tablespoon dried thyme

½ teaspoon flaky sea salt

Freshly ground black pepper

I knew I wanted to include a pork recipe in this book but I couldn't decide which one. So I went straight to the source—the mother of a French child. I asked Lucy Vanel, who runs the Plum Lyon Teaching Kitchen in Lyon, France (where some of the photos for this book were shot), what her son, Ian, would enjoy, and a nicely seared pork chop with a creamy sauce was her response. I've added some onions and apples for a hearty, yet easy-to-make dish I know kids will love. Try serving this with Silky Potato Purée (p. 112) and Buttery Green Beans with Toasted Almonds (p. 113).

1. Preheat the oven to 400°F (200°C).

2. Heat 2 tablespoons of the olive oil in a large ovenproof skillet (large enough to hold the pork chops and the apples and onions—around 10 inches/25 cm in diameter) over medium-high heat.

3. Cook the pork chops for 4 to 5 minutes on each side, until golden brown. Remove them from the skillet, place them on a plate and cover loosely with aluminum foil.

4. If there is no fat left in the pan, add the remaining 1 tablespoon of olive oil, then add the apples and onion and cook for about 5 minutes, stirring occasionally—they will just be starting to soften and brown.

5. Add the broth and use a wooden spoon to scrape up any brown bits from the bottom of the skillet. Keep those brown bits in the pan, as they add flavor to your dish.

6. Add the cream, dried thyme, salt and some pepper and stir to combine.

7. Place the pork chops back in the skillet and arrange them between the apples, onions and sauce.

8. Place the skillet in the oven and cook, uncovered, for 15 minutes, or until the pork registers 155°F (68°C) on a meat thermometer. Obviously, the cook time will depend on how thick your pork chops are.

9. Remove the skillet from the oven, cover it loosely with aluminum foil and allow to rest for 10 minutes before serving. The internal temperature of the pork should have reached 160°F (71°C) by this time.

mr. neil's roast chicken
{ poulet rôti }

Serves 4

Prep time: 25 minutes

Cook time: about 1½ hours

∽

INGREDIENTS

2–3 cups roughly chopped assorted root vegetables (carrots, parsnips, potatoes)

2 medium (12 oz/350 g total) yellow onions, thickly sliced

2 tablespoons olive oil

2 small lemons, grate the zest of one and use both for the chicken

6 sprigs fresh thyme

2 teaspoons flaky sea salt

1 teaspoon freshly ground black pepper

1 whole chicken (3 lb/1.5 kg)

2 cloves garlic, unpeeled but smashed (see sidebar)

A few sprigs fresh thyme

¼ cup (57 g) salted butter, at room temperature

1–2 teaspoons dried *Herbes de Provence* or dried thyme

Freshly ground black pepper

FOR BASTING

¼ cup (57 g) salted butter, melted

2 cloves garlic, unpeeled but smashed

One of my favorite "fast food" options in France is the rotisserie chicken and roasted potatoes that you can find in any neighborhood market. You can usually just follow your nose to find the chicken seller. Back home, it's hard to recreate the flavor of both the chicken and the potatoes, but when my partner, Neil, and I were taking some basic culinary classes, we learned to use a whole stick of butter on and under the skin of the bird to produce a remarkably crispy skin. We made this for friends, and their then 7-year-old, Charlotte, was quite entranced by the amount of butter Neil was using, declaring that she'd never seen anything like it. She dubbed this Mr. Neil's Roast Chicken. We've kept the name—for both the chicken and Mr. Neil himself—ever since.

1. Preheat the oven to 425°F (220°C).
2. Scatter the chopped vegetables in a roasting pan with the olive oil. Add the lemon zest, thyme, salt and pepper to the vegetables and, using your hands, mix until all the vegetables are coated. Make sure the vegetables are sitting evenly on the bottom of the roasting pan.
3. Pat the cavity of the bird dry using a paper towel.
4. Cut both the lemons in quarters and place them in the cavity of the bird with the smashed garlic and a few sprigs of fresh thyme. If all the lemon quarters don't fit, you can pop them in the pan with the vegetables—just don't forget to take them out when you are serving the chicken.
5. Cut about half of the butter into small pieces and place them under the skin of the bird. To do this, start at the cavity end of the chicken and slide one or two fingers between the meat and the skin. Work slowly, separating the skin from the meat as far as you can reach. Squish the butter pieces slightly and fit them under the skin as best you can.
6. Spread the remainder of the butter over the outside of the skin. The easiest way to do this is with your hands. Season the bird with the *Herbes de Provence* or dried thyme and a touch of pepper.
7. Place the bird directly on the vegetables in the roasting pan and place in the oven for 20 minutes, until the skin starts to brown nicely.

To smash a garlic clove, place it on a cutting board and place a large knife that's wider than the garlic clove flat on top of the garlic with the blade facing away from you. Use all your strength to press down until the garlic clove splits. *voila!* You've just smashed it! This is also an easy way to peel garlic.

8. Add the smashed garlic to the melted butter and place this over very low heat on the stovetop. You will use this to baste the chicken while it's roasting.

9. Turn down the oven to 400°F (200°C) and roast the chicken for 60 to 70 minutes more, or until a meat thermometer inserted into the high part of the thigh registers 165°F (74°C). Normally you can count on about 20 minutes' cook time per pound (454 g) of chicken but to be absolutely sure, a meat thermometer is the way to go!

10. While the bird is cooking, baste it every 20 minutes or so with the melted butter and smashed garlic. This will season the bird even more.

11. Once the chicken is cooked, remove it from the oven (leave the vegetables in the roasting pan), place it on a cutting board (preferably one that has a drain ridge to catch any juices), cover it loosely with aluminum foil and allow it to rest for about 10 minutes before you carve it.

12. Give the vegetables a good stir and place the roasting pan back in the oven until you are ready to serve the meal. If the vegetables are not crispy enough, you can set the broiler to high (around 400°F/200°C, if your broiler has a temperature display) and broil them for about 5 minutes, but do keep an eye on them as they might burn.

☺ Kids might be squeamish about touching raw chicken (especially when it comes to placing the lemons, garlic and herbs in the cavity and the butter under and over the skin). The more they see you doing tasks like this, though, the more normal (and less gruesome) it will appear. In the meantime, get them busy chopping the vegetables and mixing in the oil and seasoning in the roasting pan.

crispy fish with lemon zest
{ filet de poisson au citron }

Serves 4

Prep time: 15 minutes

Cook time: 12 to 16 minutes

∿

INGREDIENTS

FOR THE FISH

½ cup (75 g) all-purpose flour

1 teaspoon flaky sea salt

Freshly ground black pepper

2 eggs, lightly beaten

¾ cup (64 g) Panko breadcrumbs

A heaping ⅓ cup (30 g) freshly grated Parmigiano-Reggiano cheese

Grated zest of 1 lemon (1 tablespoon)

½ teaspoon sea salt

¼ teaspoon freshly ground black pepper

4 white fish (e.g., cod) fillets (5 oz/150 g each and ¾ inch/ 1.5 cm thick)

FOR COOKING

4 tablespoons unsalted butter

4 lemon wedges, for serving

When I was growing up in Australia, I didn't like fish, which people find odd, as Australians tend to eat a lot of fish and seafood, but as an adult, I've learned not only to tolerate but to even like some fish dishes. My favorite way to enjoy fish today is a simple preparation, similar to the classic French *sole meunière*, where the fish is lightly coated in flour then sautéed in butter and flavored with lemon and parsley. This version has lemon zest and cheese for some extra flavor. I like to serve this with Silky Potato Purée (p. 112) and Buttery Green Beans with Toasted Almonds (p. 113).

prepare the fish:

1. Whisk the flour, salt and some pepper together in a large shallow bowl or plate. Pour the lightly beaten eggs into a separate small shallow bowl. Mix the breadcrumbs, cheese, zest, salt and pepper in a third shallow bowl or plate. Prepare a clean plate to set the fish on until you are ready to cook them.
2. Dip each piece of the fish in the flour mixture, coating them evenly.
3. Dip the fish in the egg mixture, coating it evenly and draining any excess back into the bowl.
4. Dip the fish in the breadcrumb mix and press down slightly so they stick. Make sure to coat both sides.
5. Set the fish aside on the clean plate.

cook the fish:

1. Preheat the oven to 250°F (120°C). Place a large serving plate inside the oven (this will be to keep the fish warm until you've cooked it all).
2. Heat 2 tablespoons of the butter in a large nonstick skillet over medium-high heat. Once the butter has melted and is bubbling, add two pieces of fish to the pan and cook them for 3 to 4 minutes, until they are crispy and golden underneath.
3. Flip the fish and cook for a further 3 to 4 minutes, until cooked through. Transfer the fish to the warm plate and return to the oven to keep warm while you cook the remaining pieces.

4. Take some paper towel and wipe the pan clean. Melt the rest of the butter. Cook the remaining fish as described above. Serve with lemon wedges

---

☺ Kids will enjoy dipping the fish in the flour, egg and breadcrumbs. Just make sure that each bowl is large enough and that they are close together to avoid too much mess. And make sure everyone washes their hands after handling the raw fish and eggs.

buttery green beans with
toasted almonds

silky potato purée

crunchy fish cakes
{ croquettes de poisson }

Serves 4

Prep time: 30 minutes

Chilling time: 30 minutes

Cook time: 25 minutes

∿

INGREDIENTS

2 medium (10 oz/300 g total) Yukon Gold potatoes, peeled and chopped

1 (10 oz/300 g) piece skinless, boneless white fish

1 large egg

1 tablespoon smooth Dijon mustard (I prefer Maille)

½ teaspoon flaky sea salt

¼ teaspoon black pepper

2 green onions, finely sliced

1 cup (85 g) Panko breadcrumbs

6 tablespoons vegetable oil

Tartar sauce, for serving

Special equipment

3-tablespoon cookie scoop

I'm going to tell you a secret. Even though I didn't like fish when I was growing up, there was one "fish" product that I secretly loved: fish fingers! As an exchange student in Belgium, one of my host mothers asked if I ate fish. I drew her a picture of fish fingers and said "*seulement ça*" (only that). She laughed and told me these were called "*les fishsticks*." This is a more sophisticated version of those, based on a project I do with my Grade 6 French class, where we learn about Haitian food and the boys choose some dishes to research and cook. *Acras de morue* (cod fish fritter) always makes the list and every year the boys make and devour this! This recipe speaks to my youthful dislike of fish looking like fish as well as to the boys' love of fritters!

1. Place the potatoes in a large pot of cold water (just enough to cover them) over high heat. Bring the water to a boil and then cook for a further 8 to 10 minutes, or until the potatoes are fork-tender.

2. Drain the potatoes in a colander and allow to cool.

3. Meanwhile, place the fish, egg, mustard, salt and pepper in the bowl of a food processor fitted with a metal blade. Pulse the mixture three to four times, until smooth. Place the fish mixture in a large bowl and set aside.

4. Roughly mash the potatoes using a potato masher or fork, until fairly smooth. Add the potatoes and the green onions to the fish mixture and use a rubber spatula to combine.

5. Cover the mix with plastic wrap and refrigerate for 30 minutes. This will make forming the fish cakes much easier.

6. When you are ready to cook the fish cakes, preheat the oven to 250°F (120°C). Place a large serving plate inside the oven (this will be to keep the fish warm until you've cooked it all).

7. Place the breadcrumbs on a large flat plate. Set an empty plate next to it. Set a third empty plate near the stovetop where you will cook the fishcakes.

8. Use a 3-tablespoon cookie scoop to form 12 fish cakes. If you don't have a cookie scoop, you can use a ¼-cup (60 mL) measure. Fill it about three-quarters full and pack the mixture in with your fingers.

Using a cookie scoop avoids too much handling of raw fish. It also means each fish cake is a consistent size, which helps you judge their "doneness" when you are cooking them.

As you form each cake, place it in the breadcrumbs and roll it around until it's fully coated. Use your hands to slightly flatten the cakes into disks. Set them on the clean plate and continue until you have 12 cakes.

9. Heat 2 tablespoons of the oil in a medium-sized skillet over medium-high heat. Once it's hot (hint: drop a breadcrumb in the oil and if it sizzles, it's ready), place four fish cakes at a time in the skillet. Cook them for 5 to 6 minutes, flipping two to three times, until they are golden and crispy.

10. Once cooked, remove the fish cakes from the pan with a spatula and place them on the clean plate in the oven to keep warm while you cook the rest of the cakes.

11. Take some paper towel and wipe the skillet clean.

12. Heat 2 more tablespoons of the oil and repeat the process until all the fish cakes are cooked. Serve with tartar sauce.

ratatouille, three ways

Many people have perhaps heard of ratatouille (pronounced ra-ta-TOO-ee) thanks to a certain movie that came out in 2007. Said to have originated in the city of Nice, this side dish includes a combination of eggplant, tomatoes, peppers, zucchini, onions and garlic and can be eaten warm, at room temperature or cold. I've included three different preparations here to account for different levels of knife skills, so no matter how accomplished your kids are in the kitchen, there should be a recipe to suit them.

The word "ratatouille" comes from variations on the verb "touiller," which means "to mix or stir," as the original version of this dish was prepared on the stovetop.

quick stovetop ratatouille
{ ratatouille }

Serves 4 to 6

Prep time: 30 minutes

Cook time: about 40 minutes

∽

INGREDIENTS

4 tablespoons (60 mL) olive oil

1 medium (12 oz/350 g) eggplant, large dice

2 medium (10 oz/300 g total) zucchini, roughly chopped

1 large (7 oz/200 g) yellow onion, roughly chopped

3 large cloves garlic, minced

2 small (10 oz/300 g total) red or orange bell peppers, roughly chopped

1 tablespoon freshly chopped basil leaves

2 teaspoons fresh (or 1 teaspoon dried) thyme

1 teaspoon flaky sea salt

¼ teaspoon freshly ground black pepper

3 medium (1½ lb/675 g total) tomatoes, roughly chopped

⅓ cup (80 mL) water

Flaky sea salt, for seasoning

Freshly ground black pepper, for seasoning

In this version, the vegetables are par-cooked separately, then finished all together in the pot. This is a great recipe for more experienced cooks to tackle, not because it's difficult, but because it's just a little more involved.

1. In a large skillet, heat 2 tablespoons of the olive oil over medium heat. Add the eggplant and cook, stirring constantly until it just starts to brown, about 8 minutes. Remove the eggplant from the skillet and place it in a large bowl.

2. Add 2 tablespoons of olive oil to the skillet and cook the zucchini over medium heat until it just starts to brown, about 6 minutes. Remove the zucchini from the skillet and place it in the bowl with the eggplant.

3. If necessary, add a splash of olive oil to the skillet and then cook the onion and garlic until they are just starting to brown and soften, about 5 minutes.

4. Add the bell peppers, basil, thyme, salt and pepper, and continue to cook over medium heat until the peppers begin to soften and the mixture is fragrant, about 5 minutes.

5. Add the tomatoes and a splash of the water and cook the vegetables over medium heat, stirring to break down the tomatoes, about 4 minutes.

6. Once the tomatoes are starting to soften, add the eggplant and zucchini and turn down the heat to a simmer. Cover and cook for a further 10 minutes, adding a touch more water if the mixture starts to look dry.

7. Season to taste with sea salt and freshly ground black pepper before serving.

☺ Talk to your kids about why each vegetable cooks for a different amount of time (some take longer and we're trying to have all the vegetables cooked perfectly by the end of the cooking process). Younger cooks who aren't up to chopping can take charge of the pot, stirring, adding and removing vegetables.

rustic oven-baked ratatouille
{ ratatouille au four }

Serves 4 to 6

Prep time: 30 minutes

Cook time: 45 to 65 minutes

~

INGREDIENTS

1 large (7 oz/200 g) yellow onion, roughly chopped

3 large cloves garlic, minced

3 small (1 lb/454 g total) tomatoes, roughly chopped

2 small (10 oz/300 g total) red or orange bell peppers, roughly chopped

1 medium (12 oz/350 g) eggplant, large dice

2 medium (10 oz/300 g total) zucchini, roughly chopped

2 teaspoons fresh (or 1 teaspoon dried) thyme

1 tablespoon freshly chopped basil leaves

4 tablespoons olive oil

½ teaspoon flaky sea salt

¼ teaspoon freshly ground black pepper

½ cup (125 mL) water

Flaky sea salt, for seasoning

Freshly ground black pepper, for seasoning

Olive oil, for drizzling

This iteration of ratatouille is very easy and hands-off. It's well suited to those with beginner knife skills in the kitchen as the vegetables only need to be roughly chopped.

1. Preheat the oven to 400°F (200°C).
2. In a large bowl, mix the onion, garlic, tomatoes, peppers, eggplant, zucchini, thyme and basil with the oil, salt and pepper, making sure the vegetables are evenly coated.
3. Place the vegetables in a single layer in a baking dish (10 x 12 inches/25 x 30 cm) and add about ¼ cup (60 mL) of the water.
4. Cover the dish with aluminum foil and bake for 45 minutes.
5. After 45 minutes, remove the foil (if the vegetables look dry, add another ¼ cup (60 mL) of the water) and bake for a further 15 to 20 minutes, until all the vegetables are cooked through but not mushy.
6. Season with flaky sea salt and freshly ground black pepper to taste and a drizzle of olive oil before serving.

☺ Very young cooks who are not ready for chopping the vegetables in this rustic dish can help measure the herbs and spices and toss the vegetables with the oil.

ratatouille tian

{ tian }

Serves 2

Prep time: 25 minutes

Cook time: 65–75 minutes

∾

INGREDIENTS

1 small (3½ oz/100 g)
yellow onion, thinly sliced

2 cloves garlic, minced

2 tablespoons olive oil

½ teaspoon flaky sea salt

Freshly ground black pepper,
for seasoning

2 baby or 1 small (7 oz/200 g)
eggplant, thinly sliced

1 medium (5 oz/150 g) zucchini,
thinly sliced

3 Roma tomatoes (10 oz/300 g),
thinly sliced in rounds

½ teaspoon dried *Herbes de
Provence*

Olive oil, for drizzling

Flaky sea salt and freshly
ground black pepper,
for seasoning

You may not know what a *tian* is, but if you've seen the movie *Ratatouille*, you'll be familiar with a version of this presentation of vegetables sliced thinly, cooked and served in an elegant stack. The dish you see in the movie was created by Chef Thomas Keller (of The French Laundry, among other restaurants), who was a consultant for the movie. My version of those stacked vegetables is a little easier for younger or novice cooks to assemble, but once you've mastered it, you're well on your way to creating restaurant-worthy ratatouille! It's important to choose vegetables that have a similar diameter so they stack evenly in the baking dish.

1. Preheat the oven to 400°F (200°C).
2. Place the onion slices and minced garlic in the bottom of a 5- x 7-inch (13 x 18 cm) baking dish. Sprinkle with 1 tablespoon of the olive oil, the ½ teaspoon flaky sea salt and some freshly ground black pepper.
3. Stack the eggplant slices upright against the long side of the dish so they are slightly overlapping each other. They should be quite tightly packed. Follow with a row of zucchini slices, arranged in the same manner. Next, make a row of tomato slices.
4. Continue in this manner until you have no more vegetable slices left. You should have enough vegetable slices and room to make at least two rows of each vegetable.
5. Drizzle 1 tablespoon of olive oil over the vegetables, sprinkle with the *Herbes de Provence*, cover the dish with aluminum foil and bake for 45 minutes.
6. Remove the foil from the dish, drizzle with a little more olive oil and bake, uncovered, for a further 20 to 30 minutes, until the vegetables are cooked through.
7. Season to taste. Serve warm or at room temperature.

Did you know that "*tian*" is the name not only for this baked vegetable stew but also the dish it's cooked in? Traditionally, it means a shallow earthenware casserole dish, but you can use a ceramic baking dish for the same effect!

Some of my younger *petits chefs* suggested I use less leek and more potato in this recipe (because, sure, a crispy potato and cheese cake sounds pretty good too!) so feel free to switch out the leek for something else (potato or otherwise). Just make sure that the total amount of grated vegetables is between 3½ and 4 cups' worth.

crispy vegetable cakes
{ croquettes de légumes }

Serves 4 to 6

Prep time: 30 minutes

Cook time: 30 minutes

∿

INGREDIENTS

1 small (3½ oz/100 g) leek

1 large (8 oz/250 g) Yukon Gold or russet potato, peeled and grated

1 large (7 oz/200 g) zucchini, grated

3 large eggs, lightly beaten

1 cup (60 g) grated cheddar cheese

¼ cup (21 g) Panko breadcrumbs

½ teaspoon flaky sea salt

¼ teaspoon freshly ground black pepper

SPECIAL EQUIPMENT

3-tablespoon cookie scoop (optional)

Just as I was a fan of a certain brand of boxed soup when I lived in Paris, I also ate my fair share of boxed, frozen vegetable *croquettes*. In my tiny kitchen area, I had no space for any sort of equipment, so even if I had wanted to make these from scratch, I didn't have room for a box grater (seriously, my kitchen sink was next to my shower—there were no cupboards at all!). Though I did eat fresh vegetables, I never prepared them in interesting ways, which is why frozen veggie *croquettes* were so appealing. Who knew they were so easy to make at home?

1. Preheat the oven to 400°F (200°C). Prepare two baking trays with parchment paper. Place a few layers of paper towel on your countertop.
2. Prepare your leek by removing the dark green tops and the root, then slicing it open lengthwise. Rinse the leek well under cold running water to remove any dirt or sand. Dry the leek as thoroughly as possible, and then finely chop the light green and white parts.
3. Squeeze the water out of each batch of grated vegetables, using your hands. Squeeze the leeks too. Squeeze as hard as you can! Place the drained vegetables on the paper towel in a single layer. Place a couple more paper towels on top and gently pat the vegetables dry.
4. Once they are dry, place the vegetables in a large bowl. Add the eggs, cheese, breadcrumbs, salt and pepper to the vegetables and mix well to combine, using a wooden spoon or your hands.
5. Using a 3-tablespoon cookie scoop and packing the mixture in tightly, scoop out mounds of the mixture and place them about 1 inch (2.5 cm) apart on the baking trays. If you don't have a cookie scoop this size, use a ¼-cup (60 mL) measure filled about three-quarters full with the mixture, pressing it to pack it in the cup. You should have approximately 20.
6. Place the baking trays on racks in the top and bottom thirds of the oven and bake for 15 minutes, then remove the trays from the oven. Use an offset spatula to carefully flip the croquettes—they are pretty fragile at this stage—flattening them slightly as you do.
7. Bake a further 15 minutes, until the croquettes are crispy and golden on both sides.

silky potato purée
{ purée de pommes de terre }

Serves 4 to 6

Prep time: 10 minutes

Cook time: 35 minutes

INGREDIENTS

2 large (1 lb/454 g total) Yukon Gold potatoes, peeled and cut into 1-inch (2.5 cm) pieces

½ cup (125 mL) 2% milk, room temperature

¼ cup (57 g) salted butter

Flaky sea salt, for seasoning

Freshly ground black pepper, for seasoning

These are not your regular mashed potatoes. French *purée* is much looser, silkier and creamier than the mashed potatoes you're probably used to. I fell in love with these when I was living in France and had my wisdom teeth out and could eat only soft foods for a week or so. A friend suggested these would help keep my strength up, since they're loaded with milk and butter—and she was right. See photo on p. 101.

1. Place the potatoes in a large pot. Fill the pot with enough cold water to cover the potatoes. Place the pot on high heat and bring to a boil.

2. Turn down the heat to medium and cook, uncovered, for about 15 minutes after the water starts to boil. The potatoes should be fork-tender at this point. The total cooking time should be around 25 minutes. Drain the potatoes into a large colander.

3. Place a metal sieve over the top of the pot. Working in batches, scoop a couple of potato pieces at a time, and press them through the sieve, back into the pot. I like to use a rubber spatula for this job. Continue until all the potatoes are back in the pot. You can also use a ricer for this step.

4. Place the pot on low heat and slowly stir in the milk. Once you have added all the milk and it is incorporated, add the butter and stir until it has melted.

5. Taste a small spoonful of the potatoes and season them with salt and pepper to your liking. Serve immediately.

There is a well-known box mix of purée (just add milk and butter) that you can buy in France called Mousline, a play on *"(pommes) mousseline,"* which means "creamy mashed potatoes," but also "muslin" or "chiffon." Imagine the silkiness of those light materials. Now imagine silky mashed potatoes. Sounds weird, but when you see and taste this dish, you'll understand!

buttery green beans with toasted almonds
{ haricots verts aux amandes }

Serves 4 to 6

Prep time: 10 minutes

Cook time: 5 minutes

∽

INGREDIENTS

¼ cup (25 g) sliced almonds

1 lb (454 g) green beans, ends trimmed

2 tablespoons salted butter

Flaky sea salt, for seasoning

Freshly ground black pepper, for seasoning

☺ I can guarantee that even kids who say they don't like beans will want to help when it comes to tasting these beans as you're cooking them to check if they are done. It's a useful way for kids to learn how not to overcook fresh vegetables.

Real French green beans are much thinner than the ones we are used to eating in North America, so if you're lucky enough to get your hands on some, make sure you don't overcook them! I've included a foolproof way to help you in this recipe. (Hint: it involves tasting as you go.) See photo on p. 101.

1. Heat a small, nonstick skillet over medium heat.
2. Scatter the almonds in a single layer in the skillet and toast them for about 5 minutes, constantly stirring or shaking the skillet to avoid burning. Remove the skillet from the heat, quickly remove the almonds and set them aside.
3. Steam or cook the green beans in boiling water for no longer than 5 minutes. Nobody likes soggy beans. If you're not sure how long to cook them for, boil a large pot of water, add a pinch of salt and carefully add the beans. Removing one bean from the pot at a time, taste them after 2, 3, 4 and 5 minutes to see how you prefer them (it will also depend on how thick they are).
4. Drain the beans and return them to the hot pot but do not place it back on the heat. Add the butter to the pot and then the toasted almonds. Use tongs to combine them. Make sure the beans are well coated with the butter, and that the almonds are well distributed through the beans.
5. Season to taste with flaky sea salt and freshly ground black pepper before serving.

cheesy scalloped potatoes
{ gratin savoyard }

Serves 4 to 6

Prep time: 25 minutes

Cook time: 45 to 50 minutes

Rest time: 15 minutes

∾

INGREDIENTS

2 large (1 lb/454 g total)
Yukon Gold potatoes, peeled
and very thinly sliced

2 cloves garlic, minced

½ cup (125 mL) 2% milk

½ cup (125 mL) heavy (35%)
cream

½ teaspoon flaky sea salt

Freshly ground black pepper

2 tablespoons unsalted butter

1½ cups (90 g) grated
Emmenthal or Swiss cheese

Flaky sea salt, for serving

Freshly ground black pepper,
for serving

For this book, I've chosen to include the lesser-known cousin of the *gratin dauphinois*, the *savoyard*. Why? Well, it has cheese. Does there need to be more of a reason? I think everyone should have a favorite potato gratin dish in their repertoire and it's the gateway to kids learning there is more to love about potatoes than fries!

1. In a large pot, bring the potatoes, garlic, milk, cream, salt and some pepper to a simmer over medium heat. Simmer for 5 minutes then remove the pot from the heat.

2. Preheat the oven to 375°F (190°C). Grease a deep baking dish (10 x 7 x 2 inches/25 cm x 18 cm x 5 cm) with the butter.

3. Using a large slotted spoon, carefully remove half the potatoes from the warm milk mixture and place them in the baking dish, spreading them evenly across the base of the dish.

4. Pour half of the milk mixture from the pot over the potatoes and sprinkle half of the grated cheese on top.

5. Repeat these layers with the remaining potatoes and milk, finishing with the rest of the cheese.

6. Bake for 45 to 50 minutes, until the gratin is bubbling and the top is golden and crispy. If your gratin is not golden at this point, you can pop it under a broiler for 3 to 5 minutes, keeping an eye on it so it doesn't burn.

7. Remove the dish from the oven and allow to sit for 15 minutes before seasoning with flaky sea salt and freshly ground black pepper and serving. There shouldn't be too much sauce at the bottom of this dish when you serve it, so don't be tempted to skip letting it sit for the full 15 minutes before you serve it. The potatoes will continue to soak up the liquid as they sit.

The "*savoyard*" in this recipe comes from the adjective to describe people and things from the Savoie region (the Alps in southeastern France), where the food contains a lot of butter, cream, cheese and milk. You can imagine this would be a warming dish if you lived in the mountains!

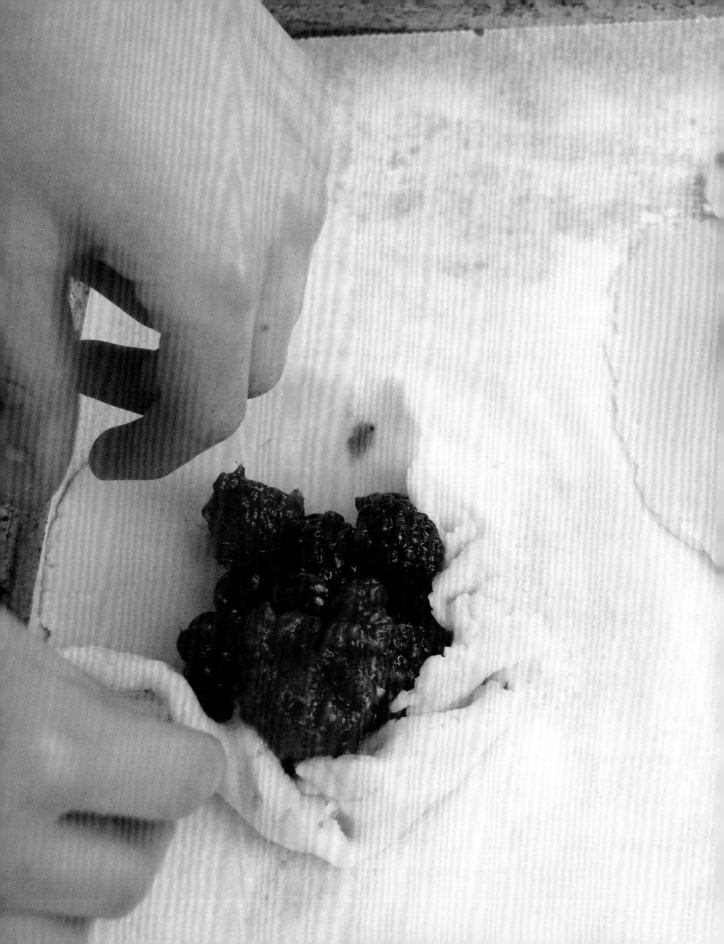

DESSERT
le dessert

When you tell people you're making a French dessert, they immediately think it must be complicated. Tell them you're making a French dessert with kids and they think you must be crazy. But do you want to know a secret? Many of those difficult-sounding desserts are actually quite simple to make, even with kids! The desserts in this chapter may have lovely, fancy French names but they rely on a few simple techniques and a few basic pantry and fridge staples. There's a mix of creamy, fruity and chocolaty recipes, so you're sure to find something for everyone. And I've included some must-know pastry recipes to set you on the road to sweet success in the French kitchen with kids!

cœur à la crème with raspberry coulis

Serves 6

Prep time: 15 minutes

Chilling time: 3 hours to overnight

∾

INGREDIENTS

FOR THE *CŒUR À LA CRÈME*

1 cup (250 mL) heavy (35%) cream

1 (8 oz/250 g) package brick-style cream cheese, at room temperature

½ cup (125 g) smooth ricotta or cottage cheese

¼ cup (35 g) icing sugar, sifted

1 teaspoon pure vanilla extract

FOR THE RASPBERRY COULIS

2 cups (200 g) fresh raspberries

¼ cup (35 g) icing sugar, sifted

1 tablespoon fresh lemon juice

SPECIAL EQUIPMENT

Six ½-cup (125 mL) heart-shaped molds (with holes in the bottom) or standard ½-cup (125 mL) ramekins; cheesecloth (if you are using the heart-shaped molds). You can buy the heart-shaped molds at specialty kitchen stores.

My mum used to make this dessert for dinner parties when I was growing up, and I remember feeling very lucky if there were leftovers. It sounded so sophisticated, and it was like nothing I'd ever had—just sweet enough, with a perfect substantial but fluffy texture that is hard to describe. It's pretty when presented in heart-shaped molds but no less delicious served in a plain ramekin. Damp cheesecloth squares are used to line the molds. While the mixture sits overnight in the fridge, the cheesecloth soaks up some of the moisture from the cream cheese, creating a solid heart that's easy to remove from the mold.

make the cœur à la crème:

1. Using handheld electric beaters, whip the cream on high speed until it forms stiff peaks, about 2 minutes.
2. In a separate bowl, (no need to rinse the beaters) beat the cream cheese and ricotta or cottage cheese with the icing sugar on medium speed until smooth. Add the vanilla and mix well.
3. Add the cream, ⅓ cup (80 mL) at a time, to the cream cheese mixture. Fold gently with a rubber spatula after each addition until thoroughly combined.

if you are using heart-shaped molds:

1. Take 18 squares of cheesecloth a bit larger than the heart-shaped molds and dampen them slightly. Squeeze out any excess moisture and line each mold with three squares.
2. Divide the mixture evenly between the molds (you can use a dessert spoon for this), rap the molds on a countertop to ensure even distribution, then layer the excess cheesecloth over the top of the mixture. Wrap the entire mold in plastic wrap and refrigerate the molds 3 hours to overnight.
3. To unmold the desserts, remove the plastic wrap, open the cheesecloth and place a plate on top of a mold. Flip the plate over so it's right side up. Remove the mold then carefully remove the cheesecloth. Repeat with the other molds.

☺ Kids will love using handheld electric beaters in this recipe, and because there are quite a few ingredients that need beating, there are enough jobs to share among a few people. Make sure kids know to hold on to the bowl with one hand and never to lift the beaters out of the bowl unless they are switched off. Younger children will enjoy portioning this between the molds or ramekins using a dessert spoon. It's best to underfill at first, then top the ramekins or molds up at the end.

if you are using ramekins:

Divide the mixture between the ramekins (you can use a dessert spoon for this), rap the ramekins on a countertop to ensure even distribution, cover with plastic wrap and refrigerate for at least 3 hours. You can eat the finished dessert straight from the ramekin.

make the raspberry coulis:

Use an immersion blender to blend the raspberries, icing sugar and lemon juice until smooth. You can strain the seeds out with a wire sieve if you like. Taste it to check if it needs a touch more sugar. If the mixture is too thick (it should be the consistency of a milkshake), you can add a couple of tablespoons of water and blitz it again.

to serve:

Drizzle the raspberry coulis around the heart shapes on the plate or on top of the ramekins.

"*Cœur à la crème*" literally means "creamy heart," hence the heart-shaped molds whose holes on the bottom allow the whey to drain out, leaving just the "heart of cream."

chocolate cœur à la crème
(aka "amanda's hearts")

Serves 6

Prep time: 15 minutes

Chilling time: 3 hours to
overnight

∽

INGREDIENTS

½ cup (90 g) semi-sweet
chocolate chips

1 cup (250 mL) heavy (35%)
cream

1 (8 oz/250 g) package brick-
style cream cheese, at room
temperature

½ cup (65 g) icing sugar, sifted

1 recipe raspberry coulis
(p. 119), for serving (optional)

SPECIAL EQUIPMENT

Six ½-cup (125 mL) heart-
shaped molds (with holes in the
bottom) or standard ½-cup
(125 mL) ramekins; cheesecloth
(if you are using the heart-
shaped molds). You can buy
the heart-shaped molds at
specialty kitchen stores.

This is a bit of a Michels family legend. It's my sister's all-time favorite dessert and she always requests it whenever she comes to stay with me or goes to Mum and Dad's for dinner. Those of us in the know don't even bother plating this in heart-shaped molds or ramekins; we just serve it in a large bowl and let people help themselves. Even though it's chocolate, it's not super sweet, so I'd recommend you serve it with raspberry coulis (p. 119).

1. Melt the chocolate in a double boiler or in a glass bowl for 2 to 3 minutes on 50% power in a microwave. Set aside to cool slightly.

2. Using handheld electric beaters on high speed, whip the cream until it forms soft peaks, about 2 minutes.

3. In a separate bowl, (no need to rinse the beaters) beat the cream cheese and icing sugar together until smooth.

4. Stir the chocolate to check that it's just barely warm, then add it to the cream cheese mixture, continuing to beat with the electric mixer until the chocolate is fully incorporated.

5. Using a rubber spatula, add the whipped cream, ⅓ cup (80 mL) at a time, to the cream cheese mixture. Fold gently until everything is well combined and you can't see any streaks of white.

6. Assemble and serve the cœur à la crème as per the directions on pages 119 and 120.

mixed berry galettes
{ petites galettes rustiques aux fruits rouges }

Makes 8 galettes

Prep time: 30 minutes

Bake time: 25 to 30 minutes

∽

INGREDIENTS

FOR THE PASTRY

1 recipe Sweet Shortcrust
Pastry (p. 168)

FOR THE FILLING

2 cups (200 g) mixed berries
(I like raspberries, blackberries
and blueberries)

2 tablespoons granulated sugar

1 tablespoon cornstarch

1 tablespoon fresh lemon juice

Grated zest from 1 small lemon
(about 1 tablespoon)

TO ASSEMBLE

1 large egg, lightly beaten for
egg wash

Granulated sugar, for sprinkling

TO SERVE

Vanilla ice cream or
Chantilly cream (p. 139)

Galettes were my introduction to the world of pastry and are still one of my favorite things to make. These single-crust pies are so easy that most kids can make them with very little supervision, and the fact that they are supposed to look rustic is a bonus for those who don't feel confident making a pie crust. The possibilities for filling a fruit galette are endless, but I've chosen mixed berries because they bake up so well and are so pretty. Once you've made one galette, you'll be hooked! Note that you need to allow time to make and chill the pastry before assembling and baking the galettes. You can make the pastry the day before if you like.

make the pastry:

1.   Prepare the sweet shortcrust pastry (p. 168).

make the filling:

1.   Combine the berries, sugar, cornstarch, lemon juice and zest in a small bowl. Stir to coat the berries thoroughly and set aside.

2.   Preheat the oven to 350°F (175°C). Line two baking trays with parchment paper.

3.   Divide the pastry into eight pieces and roll each piece out to a rough circle about 6 inches (15 cm) in diameter. If necessary, trim the rolled-out shapes with a pizza cutter so they are more or less round. Place the circles of dough on the parchment-lined baking trays. They should not be touching.

4.   Use a ¼-cup (60 mL) measure to divide the berry mixture evenly between the dough circles. Place the berries in the center of the dough and use the bottom of the measuring cup to flatten them slightly. You should leave a border of about 1½ inches (4 cm) around the edge.

If your berries are quite large, you can cut them in half. If you do that, you might not need as much of the lemon juice, since cut berries may give off more juice.

☺ This is an excellent entry-level dessert for novice bakers. Since the dough circles won't be perfect and the berries will leak some juice out onto the baking trays anyway, they will all look a little mismatched but they are meant to be "rustic" (this is what I call anything I make that doesn't turn out perfectly now!). Whenever I make these with my boys' cooking club, nobody cares how they look—the boys think they are delicious and the parents are impressed their child made pastry from scratch!

assemble the galettes:

1. Working with one circle at a time, fold the uncovered edges of dough up and around the filling, working your way around the circle. You'll end up with pleated edges that are a little rough and you might need to trim some uneven parts to ensure you don't end up with a thick area of just crust.
2. Brush the edges of each galette with a little egg wash and sprinkle the pastry with sugar.
3. Bake for 25 to 30 minutes, or until the pastry is golden and the berries are cooked.
4. Remove from the oven and place the galettes on wire racks to cool slightly. Serve warm or at room temperature with a scoop of vanilla ice cream or Chantilly cream.

The word "galette" in French can have many meanings. Here, it describes an open-faced, single-crust pie but it can also mean savory crêpes, a puff pastry dessert eaten at Epiphany (p. 149) or even shortbread cookies. Make sure you know which one you are ordering if you're in a French restaurant!

upside-down apple tartlets
{ mini tartes tatin }

Makes 12 individual tartlets

Prep time: 30 minutes

Bake time: 25 to 30 minutes

∽

INGREDIENTS

FOR THE CARAMEL

Unsalted butter, for greasing
the ramekins

¾ cup (150 g) granulated sugar

3 tablespoons water

2 tablespoons unsalted butter

FOR THE TARTLETS

2 rolls ready-made puff pastry
(1 lb/454 g in total) or 1 recipe
Rough Puff Pastry (p. 171)

3 small (1 lb/454 g in total)
Granny Smith or other tart
apples (see note)

TO SERVE

Vanilla ice cream or Chantilly
cream (p. 139)

Special equipment

12 (½-cup/125 mL) ramekins

Tarte Tatin is one of my favorite French desserts and it's always interesting to see the different ways it's presented. Because it involves hot caramel and, if you're making a full-sized tart, some precarious flipping, it's not a recipe for novice bakers (young or old), even though none of the individual components are particularly difficult. This version is made doable for everyone by being minified, though a little bit of adult supervision is required for young bakers working with caramel. The flipping of each completed tart becomes just as easy as flipping a *Crème caramel* (p. 137).

make the caramel:

1. Generously butter the 12 ramekins and place them on a baking tray.
2. Place the sugar and water in a pot, and swirl them around gently with your finger or a chopstick to make sure the water is absorbed. Place the pot over medium-high heat to melt the sugar. Do not stir.
3. Once the sugar has melted and is liquid, cook for 4 to 5 minutes, swirling the pan occasionally, but never stirring, until the caramel is a deep golden color. If sugar goes up the side of the pot while you are swirling it, use a pastry brush dipped in water to clean the sides of the pot.
4. Remove the pot from the heat and carefully add the butter. Allow it to melt without touching it (it will sizzle and bubble at first so let it settle down) and then use a wire whisk to combine all the ingredients in the pot.
5. Working quickly, pour the caramel directly into the ramekins, swirling to evenly coat the bottom of each one. Set aside.

prepare the tartlets:

1. If you are using homemade pastry, roll it out to ¼-inch (6 mm) thick. If using store-bought, unroll the pastry. Use a 3½-inch (9 cm) cookie cutter to cut 12 rounds. Place the rounds on the prepared baking tray and refrigerate until you are ready to use them.
2. Peel the apples and place them standing up on a cutting board. Starting from one side of the apple, cut them into ¾-inch-thick (2 cm)

The "*Tatin*" in this recipe's name comes from two sisters named Stéphanie and Caroline Tatin who popularized this dessert in their restaurant near Orléans in the late 1800s. It's said one of the sisters was cooking apples in butter and sugar for pie, but let them cook too long. She salvaged the dish by placing pie dough on top of the apples and finished cooking it in the oven, turning it apple-side up when she served it to diners—who loved it.

―――――――――

☺ Working with caramel requires adult supervision (especially when pouring it into the ramekins). A great way to get younger children involved with this part of the recipe is to put them on timing duty. I ask my timer to tell me when we are at 3 minutes and then again at 4 minutes. Always encourage kids to look at what's happening in the pot as it cooks. White sugar transforming into golden caramel? Best science lesson ever!

―――――――――

slices. You'll get about two slices on either side of the apple core. (You need 12 slices, so you'll need another apple if you don't cut four slices from each one.) Make sure the apple slices fit snugly in the ramekins—if they don't, you can trim them by placing the ramekin on top of the slice and carefully using a paring knife to trace around it, cutting off the excess.

assemble and bake the tartlets:

1. Preheat the oven to 400°F (200°C). Line a baking tray with parchment paper.
2. Place one apple slice directly on top of the caramel in each ramekin. If you've measured properly, the apple slice should cover nearly the entire bottom of the ramekin.
3. Remove your pastry from the fridge. Gently place one pastry disk on top of each apple slice and use your fingers or a chopstick to push it down around the apple. Poke three holes in the pastry with the tip of a sharp knife. Place the ramekins on the baking trays.
4. Bake for 25 to 30 minutes, or until the pastry is golden brown and puffed.
5. Remove the tray from the oven and use a large flat spatula to carefully lift the ramekins onto a wire rack.
6. Allow the ramekins to cool for about 5 minutes (the caramel will still be very hot at this point) before placing a small plate on top of each ramekin. Using a tea towel to hold the ramekin, hold tight and flip the plate right side up. The tartlet should fall easily onto the plate. If the apple sticks, you can gently pry it out with a small sharp knife and fit it back on the pastry—this happens more often than you would think!
7. Serve on their own at room temperature, or with ice cream or Chantilly cream.

It's important that the apples are fairly small because you'll be placing one thick slice of the apple in the ramekin, so the diameter of the apple needs to more or less match the diameter of the ramekin.

strawberry tart
{ tarte aux fraises }

Makes one (10-inch/25 cm)
tart and about 1 cup (250 mL)
crème pâtissière

Prep time: (*crème pâtissière*)
20 minutes plus 4 hours
chilling; (assembling the tart)
25 minutes

～

INGREDIENTS

FOR THE PASTRY

One (10-inch/25 cm) Sweet
Shortcrust Pastry tart shell
(see p. 168), fully baked (p. 170)

FOR THE *CRÈME PÂTISSIÈRE*

1 cup (250 mL) 2% milk

3 large egg yolks

3 tablespoons granulated sugar

¼ cup (30 g) cornstarch

1 teaspoon pure vanilla extract

2 tablespoons unsalted butter,
at room temperature and cut
into small pieces

TO ASSEMBLE

30–40 strawberries, hulled
and cut in half

Icing sugar, for dusting, or
¼ cup (60 mL) apricot jam

One of my favorite pastimes in France is to window shop . . . at fancy *pâtisseries*! I remember when I first visited Paris when I was 12, *pâtisserie* windows were more interesting to me than anything else. To my eyes, the shiny glazed fruits atop the golden pastry cream (*crème pâtissière*) were just as appealing as jewels. Though this tart has a few different components and might seem complicated, each individual component is actually really easy. You can make and bake the shell and make the *crème pâtissière* the day before you assemble.

make the crème pâtissière:

1. In a medium pot, bring the milk to a boil over medium-high heat.
2. In the meantime, whisk the egg yolks, sugar and cornstarch together in a separate medium pot.
3. Once the milk has just reached a boil, remove it from the heat and pour a couple of teaspoons of milk into the egg yolk mixture and whisk until combined. Whisk quickly so you don't scramble the eggs.
4. Slowly pour in the rest of the hot milk, whisking constantly, and place this pot over medium-high heat.
5. Continue to whisk until the mixture starts to thicken and produce large, slow bubbles. This should take 3 to 5 minutes. It should be quite thick and coat the back of a wooden spoon. Remove the pot from the heat.
6. Transfer the mixture to a clean bowl and whisk gently to cool the mixture down slightly. Let it sit for a few minutes.
7. Whisk in the vanilla and then the butter, a couple of pieces at a time, until completely incorporated.
8. Cover the *crème pâtissière* with plastic wrap, with the wrap touching the surface to prevent a skin forming, allow it to come to room temperature and then refrigerate for at least 4 hours.

The tart can be challenging to cut without breaking the strawberries. I recommend using a gentle sawing motion with a serrated knife.

assemble the tart:

1. Remove the *crème pâtissière* from the fridge and whisk it gently to loosen, as it will have thickened in the fridge.

2. Fill the baked and cooled tart shell with the *crème pâtissière*, using an offset spatula to smooth it around the shell evenly.

3. Arrange the strawberries decoratively on top of the *crème pâtissière*. You can stand them up, lie them cut side down, lie them cut side down slightly overlapping, make a couple of circles of strawberries (one outer and one inside that)—get creative!

4. Dust with icing sugar, or heat up the apricot jam for 30 to 45 seconds in the microwave to loosen it slightly, and brush the tops of the strawberries to create a quick glazed effect.

5. This is best enjoyed the day it's made. It can be kept in the fridge covered in plastic wrap for a couple of days, but the pastry will become increasingly soggy.

Did you know that "to window shop" in French is *faire du lèche-vitrine*, which literally means "to lick windows"? I'm not sure about licking windows of clothing or shoe stores, but a *pâtisserie?* Maybe!

chocolate mousse
{ mousse au chocolat }

Serves 8

Prep time: 20 minutes

Chilling time: 4 hours to
overnight

∿

INGREDIENTS

1⅓ cups (240 g) semi-sweet
chocolate chips

4 large eggs, separated

1 cup (250 mL) heavy (35%)
cream

2 tablespoons granulated sugar

TO SERVE

Chantilly cream (p. 139),
chocolate shavings or
raspberry coulis (p. 119)

SPECIAL EQUIPMENT

Eight ½-cup (125 mL) ramekins

Note that the eggs in this recipe
are not "cooked" except by the
warm chocolate. It's best to use
the freshest eggs possible.

It wouldn't be a French cookbook without a recipe for chocolate mousse.
This is one of THE classic French desserts and this recipe is adapted from
one my mum made when we were little. I'm not a fan of gelatin-thickened
mousse, so this one gets its thick texture from egg yolks cooked with
melted chocolate. Did you know "*mousse*" means "froth" or "foam"?
A sweet mousse gets its frothy or foamy texture from the beaten egg
whites or whipped cream—or in this recipe, both.

1. Melt the chocolate in a double boiler on the stovetop or in a glass
    bowl for 2 to 3 minutes on 50% power in a microwave. Set aside to
    cool slightly. It doesn't need to be completely cool, just not scorching
    hot.
2. Using handheld electric beaters on high speed, whip the egg whites to
    stiff peaks in a large metal bowl, about 3 minutes.
3. In a separate bowl, whip the cream to soft peaks using the beaters on
    high speed (no need to wash the attachments after you've whipped
    the egg whites) for 2 to 3 minutes.
4. In a third bowl, beat the egg yolks and sugar together using the
    beaters on high speed (again, no need to wash the attachments here),
    until they thicken slightly and turn pale in color, about 2 minutes.
5. Add the cooled melted chocolate to the egg yolks and continue to
    beat until thoroughly combined. The mixture may stiffen as you are
    doing this—just keep going. It will eventually be okay!
6. Using a rubber spatula, gently fold the whipped cream into the
    chocolate mixture, one-third at a time.
7. Use the rubber spatula to carefully fold in the egg whites, about one-
    third at a time. Continue to gently fold until there are no streaks of
    egg white.
8. Divide the mixture evenly between the ramekins, cover with plastic
    wrap and refrigerate for at least 4 hours, or overnight.
9. Serve as is or with a dollop of Chantilly cream, some chocolate
    shavings or a drizzle of raspberry coulis.

crème brûlée

Serves 4

Prep time: 25 minutes

Bake time: 45 to 50 minutes

Chilling time: 4 hours to overnight

∽

INGREDIENTS

3 large egg yolks

⅓ cup (67 g) granulated sugar

Seeds from ½ vanilla pod

1 cup (250 mL) heavy cream

¼ cup (60 mL) 2% milk

4–8 tablespoons granulated sugar

SPECIAL EQUIPMENT

4 shallow ½-cup (125 mL) ramekins (see sidebar)

Classic crème brûlée is made in shallow ramekins (5 inches/13 cm in diameter and 1¼ inches/3 cm high). If you do not have shallow dishes, you can use ½-cup (125 mL) ramekins but they might take longer to cook.

Crème brûlée is the dessert I'll most often order when I am in France. A simple custard with a hard caramel topping that makes a particular "thwack" sound when it's cracked with the back of a spoon, it's not only pretty to look at but also fun to eat. I prefer the classic vanilla custard, though flavored brûlées are becoming more and more popular. Many people may doubt that this is a dessert that kids can make, but it really is so simple that, except for the *brûléeing*, only a little bit of adult supervision is necessary.

1. Preheat the oven to 300°F (150°C). Fill a kettle with water and bring it to a boil. Place the ramekins in a deep-sided baking dish or roasting pan.
2. Whisk the egg yolks and sugar in a small bowl until the mixture starts to thicken slightly and become pale. Place the bowl on a damp cloth or paper towels to hold it in place when you are whisking one-handed.
3. Place the vanilla seeds in a small pot with the cream and the milk. Heat the cream and milk over medium-high heat until just about boiling (bubbles will form around the edge). Remove from the heat and allow to cool slightly.
4. Whisking gently but constantly, add about ¼ cup (60 mL) of the hot cream to the egg mixture. Once this is combined, add the rest of the hot cream into the egg, whisking until thoroughly incorporated.
5. Pour the custard into a jug (this makes it easier for kids to pour the mixture into the small ramekins), then divide the mixture evenly between the ramekins.
6. Pour the hot water from the kettle into the bottom of the baking dish, being careful not to get any in the custards, until it's about halfway up the sides of the ramekins. This is called a *bain-marie* and it cooks the custard gently.
7. Bake the custards for 45 to 50 minutes. They might still be a tiny bit jiggly in the center, but that's fine.
8. Remove the baking dish from the oven and take the ramekins out of the water bath. Use tongs or oven gloves to pick these up, as they are very hot. Place the ramekins on a wire rack to come to room temperature, then cover the dishes with plastic wrap and refrigerate until fully chilled. These can be refrigerated until you are ready to eat them, for up to 3 days.

9. When you are ready to serve, remove the chilled custards from the fridge and sprinkle 1 to 2 tablespoons of sugar on top of each one. It needs to be a thick layer, not just a sprinkle.

10. Use a small kitchen blowtorch to caramelize the sugar to a hard caramel. To do this, keep the torch moving constantly back and forth over the sugar (so no one part of it starts to burn) until it's a deep golden brown. Alternatively, you can do this under a hot broiler (about 400°F/200°C) but you will need to keep a close eye on it!

11. Allow to cool (you can even re-refrigerate) until ready to serve but don't leave them too long (i.e., overnight) in the fridge as the caramel will get soggy.

crème caramel

Serves 6

Prep time: 20 minutes

Bake time: 45 to 55 minutes

Chilling time: 4 hours to overnight

∾

INGREDIENTS

FOR THE CARAMEL

½ cup (100 g) granulated sugar

2 tablespoons water

FOR THE CUSTARD

3 large egg yolks

2 large eggs

½ cup (100 g) granulated sugar

1 cup (250 mL) 2% milk

1 cup (250 mL) heavy (35%) cream

1 teaspoon pure vanilla extract

SPECIAL EQUIPMENT

Six ½-cup (125 mL) ramekins

This is another French classic that made the rounds of the adult dinner party circuit when I was growing up. I still remember my mum making this and me thinking it was SO exotic—caramel placed on the bottom of a ramekin that flowed down over the custard when it was flipped out onto a plate? Magical! And this dessert couldn't be simpler. Even young bakers should be able to manage most of this on their own, apart from making the caramel and using the stovetop.

make the caramel:

1. Place the sugar and water in a pot, and swirl them around gently with your finger or a chopstick to make sure the water is absorbed. Place the pot over medium-high heat. Do not stir.
2. Once the sugar has melted and is liquid, cook for 4 to 5 minutes, swirling the pan occasionally, but never stirring, until the caramel is a deep golden color. If sugar goes up the side of the pan when you are swirling, use a pastry brush dipped in water to clean the sides of the pot.
3. Pour the caramel directly into the ramekins, swirling to evenly coat the bottom of each one. Place the ramekins in a deep-sided baking dish or roasting pan, and place this on the countertop close to the oven.

make the custard:

1. Preheat the oven to 300°F (150°C). Fill a kettle with water and bring it to a boil.
2. In a large, heatproof bowl, using handheld electric beaters, beat the egg yolks, eggs and sugar on high speed until pale and starting to thicken slightly, 2 to 3 minutes. Place the bowl on a damp cloth or paper towels to hold it in place later when you are whisking one-handed.
3. Meanwhile, in a medium-sized pot, heat the milk and cream over medium-high heat. Bring this to a simmer (do not boil) and immediately remove from the heat.

☺ Though this recipe does involve caramel-making that will need to be supervised by an adult, there is still plenty for younger children to do here. Teach younger cooks how to separate egg yolks from the whites. Have them catch the cracked egg in one hand and let the white seep through their fingers into a bowl so that they end up with just the yolk (it might take a bit of practice so make sure you have a few extra eggs on hand). Whisking sugar and egg yolks together is a good activity to keep little hands busy, as is pouring the mixture into the ramekins. Once the custards have cooked and cooled, the flipping process is absolutely kid-friendly—especially if you demonstrate one first. If they are cooked properly, the custards should easily flip so the caramel is on top.

4. Slowly pour about one-quarter of the hot cream into the egg mixture, whisking constantly so you don't scramble your eggs! Once this is completely combined, add the rest of the hot cream and the vanilla, whisking constantly.

5. Pour the custard into a large jug (this makes it easier for kids to pour the mixture into the small ramekins).

6. Pour the mixture into the ramekins. Pour the boiling water from the kettle into the baking dish, being careful not to get any water in the custard, until it's about halfway up the sides of the ramekins. This is called baking in a *bain-marie* and it cooks the custard gently.

7. Carefully place the baking dish in the oven and bake for 45 to 55 minutes. The outside of the custard should be cooked but the center of the custards might still be a little jiggly.

8. Remove the dish from the oven and, using rubber-tipped tongs or a flat spatula, remove the ramekins from the boiling water. Place them on a wire rack to come to room temperature.

9. Cover each ramekin in plastic wrap and refrigerate until chilled, at least 4 hours or overnight (these will keep for a day or so in the fridge).

10. When you are ready to serve, remove the ramekins from the fridge and, one by one, place each one in a dish of lukewarm water for a minute or so.

11. Run the blade of a small knife around the edge of the custard, place a small plate on top of each ramekin and, holding tight, flip the plate. The custard should fall easily onto the plate but if not, you can shake the plate vertically until you hear it drop.

cream puffs
{ profiteroles }

Makes about 50 puffs

Prep time: 45 minutes

Bake time: 25 minutes

~

INGREDIENTS

FOR THE PUFFS

1 recipe Choux Pastry (p. 175)

FOR THE CHANTILLY CREAM

1 cup (250 mL) heavy (35%) cream

¼ cup (35 g) icing sugar, sifted

1 teaspoon pure vanilla extract

FOR THE CHOCOLATE GLAZE

¾ cup (135 g) semi-sweet chocolate chips

¼ cup (57 g) unsalted butter

1 tablespoon light corn syrup or liquid glucose (found at health food stores)

SPECIAL EQUIPMENT

Large (18-inch/45 cm) piping bag fitted with a plain (¾-inch/ 2 cm) piping tip

There's nothing more lovely than a profiterole. Light, airy pastry, tradition-ally filled with sweetened whipped cream and topped with shiny chocolate glaze, these sweet treats have been enjoying some attention in Paris recently. Some of my favorite stores that specialize in this classic dessert include Popelini, Profiterole Chéri, Odette and La Maison du Choux, but the good news is that you don't have to go to Paris to enjoy one!

bake the puffs:

1. Prepare the choux pastry (p. 175).
2. Preheat the oven to 400°F (200°C). Line two baking trays with parchment paper.
3. Scrape the choux pastry dough into the prepared piping bag and, piping from the top to form a shape not unlike a chocolate kiss, pipe rounds of 1½ inches (4 cm) in diameter, about 1½ inches (4 cm) apart. You're looking to form puffs the size of walnuts in their shells. If you don't have a piping bag, you can use a teaspoon (the kind you stir your tea with, not the measure) to scoop up a heaping spoonful of the mixture and then use a second teaspoon to push it off onto the baking tray, forming a ball as you do.
4. Dip your finger in water and use it to smooth the top of each puff, removing any tips that have formed.
5. Place the trays on racks in the top and bottom thirds of the oven and bake for 25 minutes, switching the trays from top to bottom and turning them from front to back halfway through the cook time to ensure even baking.
6. Remove the trays from the oven, place the puffs directly on wire racks and allow them to cool completely before filling. You can store the unfilled puffs in airtight containers for a few days, but they will become increasingly less crisp. See recipe notes about freezing uncooked choux dough (p. 85).

If you are piping the cream into the puffs, you don't need a piping tip. Simply stand the piping bag up in a tall glass and spoon the cream into it. Close the top of the bag and twist the bag to seal it. Holding the bag facing up, snip the end off with a pair of scissors (if using a disposable bag). You can also use a large resealable plastic bag for this purpose, but make sure you have pressed any excess air out of the bag, otherwise when you squeeze the cream out, the bag might burst, splattering cream all over you!

make the chantilly cream:

1. Combine the cream, icing sugar and vanilla in a large metal bowl.
2. Using handheld electric beaters on high speed, whip the cream until it forms stiff peaks, 4 to 6 minutes. To check if it's ready, lift the beaters out of the cream—the cream should stand up in peaks in the bowl. Place the cream in the fridge until you are ready to use it.

make the chocolate glaze:

1. Place the chocolate, butter and corn syrup in a metal bowl set over a pot of gently simmering water, stirring occasionally, until melted. You can also do this in a microwave in a microwave-safe bowl at 50% heat, in increments of 1 to 2 minutes, until it's melted.
2. Remove the bowl from the heat or microwave and stir until completely smooth.

assemble the profiteroles:

1. Cut the cooled puffs in half using a small serrated knife and line them up on the baking tray with the top halves facing down (this will help make sure you put the filling only in the bottom halves of the puffs).
2. Spoon or pipe the Chantilly cream into the bottom halves of the puffs (see the sidebar).
3. Dip the top halves of the puffs in the chocolate glaze, gently shaking off any excess, and place them on top of the cream. *Voilà!*

When my Grade 4 students researched profiteroles, one of their questions was "Where does the name come from?" We managed to find out that the word *"profiterolle"* ("little profit") was used in the 16th century to mean a tip given to chamber maids that consisted of small bread rolls cooked in ashes. Over the years, the rolls evolved, with royal pastry chefs stuffing them with sweet fillings like jelly. The invention of choux pastry is attributed to Catherine de Medici's pastry chefs (one of whom, Popelini, gives his name to a store in Paris today that sells cream puffs in various flavors). Finally, in the 19th century, the profiterole began to resemble what we know today.

éclairs

Makes about 20 éclairs

Prep time: 45 minutes

Chilling time: 4 hours to overnight

Bake time: 25 minutes

∽

INGREDIENTS

FOR THE *CRÈME PÂTISSIÈRE*

1½ cups (375 mL) 2% milk

4 egg yolks

¼ cup (50 g) granulated sugar

⅓ cup (40 g) cornstarch

1 teaspoon pure vanilla extract

2 tablespoons unsalted butter, at room temperature and cut into small pieces

FOR THE PASTRY

1 recipe Choux Pastry (p. 175)

FOR THE FONDANT GLAZE

3 cups (390 g) icing sugar, sifted

¼ cup (60 mL) warm water

1 tablespoon light corn syrup or liquid glucose (found at health food stores)

Food coloring (powder or gel)

In recent years, all over France but especially in Paris, éclairs have really come into their own as an "it" dessert. There are éclair cookbooks and even stores dedicated to selling just éclairs. Two of my favorites are L'Éclair de Génie (which opened a store in Canada in 2017) and L'Atelier de l'Éclair. This is a sophisticated-looking dessert but it's not that difficult to put together. The base components are easy to make, and once you've mastered this classic version, you can play with different flavor combinations.

make the crème pâtissière:

1. In a medium pot, bring the milk to a boil over medium-high heat.
2. In the meantime, whisk the egg yolks, sugar and cornstarch together in a separate medium pot, not on the heat.
3. Once the milk has just reached a boil, pour a couple of teaspoons of the hot milk into the egg yolk mixture and whisk until combined.
4. Slowly pour in the rest of the hot milk, whisking constantly, and place the egg mixture pot over medium-high heat, continuing to whisk.
5. Continue to whisk until the mixture starts to thicken and produce slow large bubbles. This should take 3 to 5 minutes. It should be quite thick and coat the back of a wooden spoon. Remove the pan from the heat.
6. Transfer the *crème* to a clean bowl and whisk gently to cool the mixture down slightly. Let it sit for a few minutes to cool further.
7. Whisk in the vanilla, then the butter, a couple of pieces at a time, until completely incorporated.
8. Cover the *crème* with plastic wrap. The wrap should touch the surface to prevent a skin forming. Allow to come to room temperature, then refrigerate for at least 4 hours, or until you are ready to use it (you can keep it in the fridge for up to 3 days if you are not using it immediately). Before you fill the éclairs, give the *crème* a whisk to loosen it.

FOR DECORATING

Sprinkles (optional)

SPECIAL EQUIPMENT

Large (18-inch/45 cm) piping
bag fitted with an open star
(¾-inch/2 cm) piping tip

☺ Éclairs and profiteroles
are both such doable recipes
for kids, though it may look like
there are a lot of stages. The
choux pastry itself is simple
and doesn't need any special
equipment—in fact, beating the
eggs into the dough is a great
task to divide between a few
pairs of hands. The *crème
pâtissière* requires some adult
supervision (and a close eye on it
so it doesn't become scrambled
egg crème!) but it's not actually
terribly complicated. Obviously
the most fun part for kids will be
assembling the profiteroles and
éclairs, a task particularly well
suited to younger bakers, but fun
for everyone.

bake the éclairs:

1. Prepare the choux pastry (p. 175).
2. Preheat the oven to 400°F (200°C). Line two baking trays with parchment paper.
3. Place the choux pastry into the prepared piping bag.
4. Pipe éclairs about 5 inches (13 cm) long and ¾ inch (2 cm) wide with at least 2 inches (5 cm) in between each éclair.
5. Place the trays on racks in the top and bottom thirds of the oven and bake for 25 minutes, switching the trays from top to bottom and turning them from front to back halfway through the cook time to ensure even baking.
6. Remove the trays from the oven, place the éclairs directly on wire racks and allow them to cool completely before filling. You can store the unfilled éclairs in airtight containers for a few days, but they will become increasingly less crisp. See recipe notes about freezing uncooked choux dough on p. 85.

make the fondant glaze:

1. Mix the icing sugar, water and corn syrup together in a medium pot. It will be very thick at this point.
2. Heat the mixture over very low heat on the stove until it is the consistency of heavy cream and has reached a temperature of about 100°F (37°C), measured with a digital thermometer. You don't want to heat the mixture too much at this stage, as it might cause it to set as grainy rather than glossy.
3. Divide the warm fondant between some smaller microwave-safe bowls. Add a small amount of food coloring to each bowl and stir to combine. Set aside at room temperature until you are ready to use it.

assemble the éclairs:

1. Using a small serrated knife, slice the éclairs in half as you would a dinner roll. Line them up on the baking tray with the top halves facing down. This will help make sure you only fill the bottom halves of the éclairs.

2. Spoon or pipe the *crème pâtissière* onto the bottom halves of the éclairs.

3. Dip the top halves of the éclairs in the fondant glaze, gently shaking off any excess and perhaps smoothing it with an offset spatula or a knife, and place on top of the *crème pâtissière*. For a fun look, top them with sprinkles! (The fondant icing may thicken up while it sits. If it does, simply pop the bowls in the microwave and warm them in increments of 30 seconds until the mixture is the consistency of thick cream again. You may have to do this a few times as you are topping the éclairs.)

SPECIAL OCCASIONS
pour les grandes occasions

EPIPHANY {ÉPIPHANIE}

CANDELMAS {LA CHANDELEUR}

FOR BIRTHDAYS AND OTHER PARTIES {POUR LES FÊTES}

In this chapter, you'll learn to make four desserts commonly eaten in French homes to celebrate certain times of the year. Even if you don't celebrate these holidays or festivals yourself, it's fun to learn about other cultures' traditions through the food they eat to celebrate them. Don't be put off by how fancy these desserts look, either. While they might look complicated, when you read the recipes closely you'll see that they are all fairly simple to make. Some of them may require a little patience (there's a lot of "waiting time" involved with baking, but you can use that time to clean the kitchen!) and you'll even put some of your craft skills to work. Get used to answering the question "Are you sure you didn't buy this?"

galette des rois
{ la galette des rois à la crème d'amande }

Serves 6 to 8

Prep time:
Active time: 10 minutes
(almond cream); 30 minutes
(assembly)
Chilling time: 1 hour to
overnight (almond cream);
1 hour (assembly)

Bake time: 35 to 40 minutes

INGREDIENTS

FOR THE ALMOND CREAM

¼ cup (57 g) unsalted butter,
at room temperature

¼ cup (50 g) granulated sugar

1 large egg, at room
temperature

1 teaspoon pure vanilla extract

½ cup (50 g) almond meal

¼ teaspoon fine sea salt

FOR THE PASTRY

2 rolls store-bought puff pastry
(1 lb/454 g), thawed but chilled,
or 1 recipe Rough Puff Pastry
(p. 171), chilled

January 6 is the Feast of Epiphany, celebrating the arrival of the Three Kings in Bethlehem to visit the baby Jesus. The Kings give their name to the pastry treat that is widely eaten in France to celebrate this day—*la galette des rois*. This version is perhaps the best known. It's a flaky puff pastry cake filled with almond cream and a special surprise! Note that if you make your own rough puff pastry (p. 171) for this, it's a good idea to start it the day before.

make the almond cream:

1. Using handheld electric beaters on high speed, beat the butter and sugar until smooth and creamy, about 3 minutes.
2. Add the egg and vanilla and beat until well combined. Your mixture may look a little curdled, but that's okay.
3. Using a rubber spatula, gently fold in the almond meal and salt until you have a smooth paste. It will be quite stiff.
4. Cover the almond mixture with plastic wrap and refrigerate for at least 1 hour, or overnight.

prepare the pastry:

1. If using store-bought pastry, roll out the pastry and cut two circles (10 inches/25 cm and 9 inches /23 cm in diameter). Place them, separated and sandwiched by parchment paper, on a baking tray in the fridge until you are ready to use them.
2. If using rough puff pastry, remove the pastry from the fridge and cut it in half.
3. Shape one of the halves into a disk and roll it between two sheets of parchment paper to make a circle that measures about 10 inches (25 cm) in diameter. Place the pastry circle (still sandwiched between the sheets of parchment) on a baking tray in the fridge while you work with the second piece of pastry.

1 large egg, lightly beaten,
for egg wash

1 tablespoon heavy (35%)
cream

1 dried bean or *fève*
(see sidebar)

1 paper crown

‖

"*Fève*" means "bean," and originally the *galette des rois* contained a dried bean instead of the porcelain or plastic trinkets you find in France these days. You might also hear the trinkets hidden in the *galette* referred to as *santons*, which means "little saints." This refers to traditionally terracotta (nowadays porcelain) figurines, which represent the nativity characters and which can still sometimes be found inside *galette des rois* today. The *galette des rois* is topped off with a paper crown. Tradition says that the youngest person in the room sits under the table and names who receives each slice (so there's no way they can see who gets the *fève*). The person who finds the *fève* in their slice will wear the crown and be king (or queen) for the day.

4. Shape the second half of the pastry into a disk and roll it between two sheets of parchment paper to a circle that measures about 9 inches (23 cm) in diameter. Place the pastry circle (still sandwiched between the sheets of parchment) in the fridge.

assemble the galette:

1. Whisk the egg and the cream together to make your egg wash. Remove the smaller pastry circle from the fridge and place it on a baking tray. Peel off the top layer of parchment, leaving the bottom parchment in place.

2. Spread the almond cream in the center of the pastry circle, leaving a border of about 1 inch (2.5 cm) around the edge. Place the dried bean or *fève* in the almond cream so that it's completely covered. You can use an offset spatula to help spread the cream evenly over the pastry. Brush the edge of the pastry circle with the egg wash, making sure to keep the egg on the pastry and not dripping down the edges. (If you let the egg wash drip down, your puff pastry might not puff.)

3. Remove the larger pastry disk from the fridge, peel it off the parchment and carefully place it on top of the almond cream, lining up the edges of both pastry circles. (The larger size means the pastry covers the bottom circle of pastry all the way to the edges, even with the almond cream on top.) Gently press the edges down on both the egg-washed border and the almond cream with your hands, then use your fingertips (or the tines of a fork) to lightly press around the edges of the *galette* to seal it.

4. Use the back of a small, sharp knife to score a pattern on top of the pastry. You can make a grid pattern or a sun pattern. For the sun, start from the center of the *galette* and trace a slightly curved line to the very edge of the pastry. Do not cut through the pastry. Turn the *galette* slightly clockwise and repeat, until you have scored the top of the *galette* all over. Brush the top of the *galette* with more egg wash, making sure it doesn't drip down the sides.

5. Place the baking tray with the *galette* in the fridge for 30 minutes.

6. Preheat the oven to 375°F (190°C).

7. Remove the *galette* from the fridge, brush it one more time with egg wash, then bake for 35 to 40 minutes, until the pastry is puffed and golden brown.

8. Place the *galette* on a wire rack and allow it to come to room temperature before serving topped with a paper crown!

king cake
{ gâteau des rois briochée }

Serves 10

Prep time: 20 minutes

Proofing time: 2 hours

Bake time: 30 to 35 minutes

∿

INGREDIENTS

FOR THE PASTRY

1 recipe Simple Brioche Dough
(p. 164)

1 dried bean or *fève* (see
sidebar on p. 150)

1 large egg, lightly beaten, for
egg wash

FOR THE ASSEMBLY

½ cup (125 mL) apricot jam

1–2 tablespoons boiling water

Approx. ½ cup (75 g) finely
chopped glacé (candied) fruit

¼ cup (50 g) pearl sugar

1 paper crown

Although Epiphany is celebrated all over France, if you're in the south of the country, you might notice a different type of sweet treat being eaten on this day. Especially in Provence, the *gâteau des rois briochée*, a ring of fruit-filled or fruit-topped brioche (also containing the *fève*—see p. 150) is more customary than the *galette des rois* (p. 149). This is a little more involved than the puff pastry version but no less doable. You can prepare your brioche dough (p. 164) the day before to simplify the process, if you like.

make the pastry:

1. Line a baking tray with parchment paper.
2. If the brioche dough has rested in the fridge overnight, remove it from the fridge and let it sit for about 15 minutes so it's not super cold to work with. It's not a light and airy dough, and it will feel like a substantial one. The dough should weigh around 2 lb (900 g).
3. Cut the dough into ten equal parts. If you want the pieces the exact same size, weigh each piece and add or remove dough as necessary until they are even. Shape each piece into a ball, placing the bean or *fève* inside one of them.
4. Cup your hand around one piece of dough and roll it around your work surface to form a smooth ball. Place all the dough balls in a tight circle, seam side down, on the prepared baking tray.
5. Cover the dough with a clean tea towel and leave to proof in a warm place for 2 hours. It will not rise a lot in this time, so don't worry if you don't see much difference.
6. About 30 minutes before the brioche is ready to bake, preheat the oven to 400°F (200°C). Brush the tops of the dough balls with the egg wash.
7. Bake for 30 to 35 minutes, or until the top of the brioche is golden.
8. Remove the tray from the oven and place the tray on a wire rack to cool completely.

The ring of brioche balls should be about 8 inches (20 cm) in diameter on the outside and 4 inches (10 cm) on the inside. If you like, place a cake ring around the outside of the rolls or place a smaller ring inside to help the brioche remain in a ring shape.

assemble the brioche:

1. Mix the apricot jam with the boiling water. Brush the top and sides (inside and outside) of the cooled brioche with the jam.

2. Scatter the glacé fruit and pearl sugar over the top of the brioche, pressing gently with your fingertips so that it sticks into the jam.

3. Place the paper crown on top of the brioche and serve! This is best enjoyed the day it's made, although you can store leftovers in airtight containers or resealable plastic bags for up to 3 days. They'll taste great toasted too!

crêpes

Makes about 8 crêpes

Prep time: 10 minutes

Cook time: 5 minutes
per crêpe

∽

INGREDIENTS

²⁄₃ cup (100 g) all-purpose flour

¼ teaspoon fine sea salt

1¼ cups (310 mL) 2% milk

1 large egg, lightly beaten

2 tablespoons unsalted butter,
melted then cooled

Vegetable oil, to grease the
pan for the first crêpe

Sugar, jam, Chantilly cream
(page 139) or lemon juice, for
serving

You might think that the French traditionally eat crêpes on Mardi Gras, the day before Ash Wednesday, which signals the start of Lent. In fact, in France, crêpes are eaten on La Chandeleur, or Candlemas, which is celebrated by Catholics on February 2, 40 days after Christmas. It's also known as *la fête de la lumière* or the Festival of Light ("*chandeleur*" comes from the word "*chandelle*," which means candle) and it marks the day Mary was allowed back into the synagogue after giving birth to Jesus. Nowadays, it's celebrated in France by eating crêpes! Tradition says that if you hold a coin in the hand you write with while you flip the crêpe in the pan with the other and you manage to catch the crêpe, your family will enjoy a prosperous year.

1. Place the flour and salt in a large bowl. Slowly pour in the milk, whisking constantly.

2. Once all the milk is mixed in, add the lightly beaten egg and whisk until there are no lumps.

3. Add the melted, cooled butter and whisk gently to combine. You can use this batter straight away or place it in the fridge until you're ready to use it. If you place it in the fridge, you'll need to give it a good whisk before you use it.

4. When you are ready to make the crêpes, lightly oil a 10-inch (25 cm) preferably nonstick skillet. Pour a little bit of vegetable oil on a paper towel and coat the entire pan with it, then place the pan on medium-high heat.

5. To tell whether the pan is ready, put a drop of the batter in—literally, a drop will do—and if it starts to sizzle and cook, you are ready to cook!

6. Use a ¼-cup (60 mL) measure for the batter. Hold the skillet with one hand and lift it off the heat while you pour the batter into the center of the pan. Quickly swirl the skillet around in a circular motion to distribute the batter evenly.

7. Place the skillet back on the heat and cook the crêpe for about 2 minutes. The top will bubble and the bottom will be golden brown and lacy-looking.

8. Using a plastic spatula, flip the crêpe over and cook for a further 2 minutes.

☺ I've made this recipe with 17 nine-year-old boys in our school science lab and was impressed with the beautiful crêpes they produced. You might need to demonstrate the technique, but let kids have a go at this and I know you'll be pleasantly surprised. One trick that kept everyone focused was that each group only had a certain amount of batter and knew how many crêpes it *should* make. The boys took the challenge to not waste any batter or mess anything up very seriously! Having clear expectations about certain steps in a recipe helps kids stay on track and, ultimately, experience more success.

9. Place the cooked crêpes on a warm plate and cover each one with a sheet of paper towel to keep it warm and separated from the other crêpes while you cook the rest of the batter. You may need to add a touch more oil to the pan during the process; if so, repeat Steps 4 and 5.

10. Serve these sprinkled with sugar, jam, Chantilly cream (p. 139) or a squeeze of lemon juice. Once cooked and cooled to room temperature, the crêpes will keep overnight in the fridge tightly wrapped in plastic. You can reheat them for a few minutes in a skillet over medium heat. They won't be as good the next day, but they will be better than no crêpe at all!

choux puff tower
{ pièce montée }

Serves 20 as part of a dessert table

Prep time: 1 hour

Bake time: 25 minutes

Assembly: 30 minutes

∾

INGREDIENTS

FOR THE PUFFS

1½ recipes Choux Pastry
(p. 175)

FOR THE CONE

1 piece of construction paper
(22 x 14 inches/56 x 36 cm)

Clear tape

Scissors

Cake stand

FOR THE FONDANT

3 cups (390 g) icing sugar,
sifted

¼ cup (60 mL) warm water

1 tablespoon light corn syrup
or liquid glucose (found at
health food stores)

Food coloring (powder or gel)

Maybe you've seen the *pièce montée*'s more famous cousin, the *croquem-bouche*, traditionally served as a wedding cake in France. It's a pyramid or tower of choux puffs, each one filled with pastry cream, dipped in hard caramel and decorated with spun sugar. None of the elements of *croquembouche* are complicated, but I've opted for a simpler, but no less fun, version here with no pastry cream filling and no caramel. This is a great activity for a birthday (or any occasion) party. If you make the choux puffs and top them with the fondant icing in advance, you can let the kids assemble the tower and then eat it!

bake the puffs:

1. Prepare the choux pastry (p. 175).
2. Preheat the oven to 400°F (200°C). Line three baking trays with parchment paper.
3. Scrape the choux pastry dough into the prepared piping bag and, piping from the top to form a shape not unlike a chocolate kiss, pipe rounds of 1 to 1½ inches (2.5 to 4 cm) in diameter, and about 1½ inches (4 cm) apart. You're looking to form puffs the size of walnuts in their shells. If you don't have a piping bag, you can use a teaspoon (the kind you stir your tea with, not the measure) to scoop up a heaping spoonful of the mixture and then use a second teaspoon to push it off onto the baking tray, forming a ball as you do. You should have about 80 puffs.
4. Dip your finger in water and use it to smooth the tops of each puff, removing any tips that have formed.
5. Place the trays in the oven evenly spaced out and bake for 25 minutes, switching the trays around on the racks and turning them from front to back halfway through the cook time to ensure even baking.
6. Remove the trays from the oven, place the puffs on wire racks and allow them to cool completely before filling.

FOR ASSEMBLY

Approx. 1 cup (50 g) mini marshmallows

1 tablespoon water

SPECIAL EQUIPMENT

Digital candy thermometer

Large (18-inch/45 cm) piping bag fitted with a plain (³/₄-inch/2 cm) piping tip

I've opted to leave the choux puffs empty because it's a little bit complicated to fill them and keep them intact. If you want to add some more color to your choux tower, you can "glue" whole raspberries in between the choux puffs using the fondant icing. Place them round side out for a pretty pop of red between the pastel choux puffs.

make the cone:

1. Roll the construction paper up into a cone shape about 13 inches high and 6 inches in diameter at the base (33 x 15 cm). Use clear tape to stick the paper together.

2. Trim the bottom of the cone so it sits flat on the cake stand.

make the fondant:

1. Mix the icing sugar, water and corn syrup together in a medium pot. It will be very thick at this point.

2. Heat the icing sugar mixture gently on the stove until the mixture is the consistency of heavy cream and has reached a temperature of about 100°F (37°C), measured with a digital thermometer. You don't want to heat the mixture too much at this stage as it might cause it to set as grainy rather than glossy.

3. Divide the warm fondant between some small microwave-safe bowls. Add a small amount of food coloring to each bowl and stir to combine. Set aside until you are ready to use.

assemble the choux puff tower:

1. Dip each of the cooled choux puffs in one of the colored fondants and place them back on the parchment-lined baking trays to set (you can use the same parchment that they baked on). The fondant may thicken up while it sits. If it does, simply pop the bowls in the microwave and reheat for a few seconds, until the mixture is the consistency of thick cream again. You may have to do this a few times as you are topping the puffs.

2. When all the puffs are topped and set, you can start to stick them on the paper cone. Place the mini marshmallows and water in a microwave-safe bowl and heat in the microwave in increments of 15 seconds until the marshmallows are melted. Give this mixture a good stir. You may need to repeat this process as you're sticking the puffs on.

3. Dip the bottom of each puff into the melted marshmallows, or spread the mixture on the bottom of each puff with a butter knife. Place the puffs, "glue" side down, around the paper cone, starting at the bottom. You'll need to hold the puffs in place until they stick. Once you've reached the top, you're ready to serve!

BASIC PASTRY RECIPES
recettes de base de pâtisserie

For so many years I was afraid of pastry and never even attempted making it. I had it in my head that homemade pastry was "difficult" and that I was much better off sticking with the store-bought kind. That all changed in the summer of 2012, when I met Kate Hill at the Kitchen at Camont in Gascony, in southwest France. Over a magical weekend of cooking, baking and food photography, I noticed how Kate would breeze into the kitchen, whip up some shortcrust pastry and use it in a tart that would taste spectacular, due in part to the buttery flakiness of her homemade pastry. I watched Kate closely as she made her pastry and was amazed to see how easy it was. Encouraged, I started experimenting and discovered that not only is making pastry easy, it's fun! And it's a perfect activity for kids. Where possible, I've given options to use food processors, handheld electric beaters and stand mixers, but I always encourage beginner pastry-makers to start out doing as much as they can by hand so they can learn what the different stages of pastry feel like. The pastry-making sessions in my cooking club are always some of the most popular, so go on, get in the kitchen with your kids and give it a go!

simple brioche dough
{ pâte à brioche }

Makes 12 breakfast rolls or
1 large brioche

Prep time: 20 minutes

Proofing time: 1 hour at room
temperature (or overnight in
the fridge plus 2 hours at room
temperature the next day)

INGREDIENTS

3⅓ cups (500 g) all-purpose
flour

¼ cup (50 g) granulated sugar

1½ teaspoons instant yeast

1 teaspoon fine sea salt

1 cup (250 mL) 2% milk

1 large egg, lightly beaten

½ cup (113 g) unsalted butter,
melted and slightly cooled

All-purpose flour, for sprinkling

½ tablespoon vegetable oil,
for the proofing bowl

This is a lovely buttery, sweet dough that works well for items like Breakfast Rolls (p. 31) or larger brioche like the *Gâteau des rois briochée* (p. 153). You can make this dough and use it immediately once it's proofed for an hour or you can pop it in the fridge overnight and let it proof at room temperature for 2 hours before you use it.

1. Place the flour, sugar, yeast and salt in a large bowl. Whisk to combine.
2. Heat the milk in a small pot over low heat to 110°F (43°C), measuring the temperature with a digital thermometer. If you are using a microwave, use a microwave-safe bowl and start with 30 seconds on high. If it's not hot enough, you can continue to heat in increments of 15 seconds, to be sure not to overheat.
3. Pour the warm milk into the dry ingredients and stir with a wooden spoon until the dry ingredients are just combined. The mixture will be a little shaggy and dry at this stage.
4. Whisk the beaten egg and melted butter together to combine and then stir them carefully into the dough until the mixture comes together and all the dry ingredients are fully combined. This will be a fairly sticky mixture at first. I use a rubber spatula to press the dry ingredients into the dough when it seems like the wooden spoon can't be of any more help.
5. Bring the dough together with your hands, still in the bowl, and start to knead until the dough comes together fully and starts to feel smooth.
6. Place the dough on a lightly floured surface, sprinkle it with a little more flour and start to knead. You'll be kneading for 5 full minutes continually, so it's a good idea to share this task with another person! To knead, you'll need to stretch the dough away from you with the heel of one hand and pull it toward you with the other hand and then roll the dough into a ball. Knead a few times with the heel of your hand and then stretch the dough again. Continue like this for 5 minutes. The dough will be smooth and elastic by the time you're done.

☺ This is a nice entry-level bread recipe to make with kids because, unlike some doughs, it can be made in a morning and be ready for lunch. There is also a lot of kneading, rolling and shaping here to keep small hands busy. Don't worry too much about technique with the kneading, it's more about working the dough for a full 5 minutes than following a precise method. If you are working with very young children, know that you'll be doing most of the actual work but even with minimal kneading, it's great for them to learn what a dough should feel like.

7. Pour around ½ tablespoon of vegetable oil into a large metal or glass bowl and use a paper towel to evenly coat the insides of the bowl with the oil. Place the dough in the bowl, cover tightly with plastic wrap and leave it to proof at room temperature for 1 hour. If you are not using the dough immediately, place the bowl in the fridge overnight. Note that if you are putting the dough in the fridge, it will also need around 2 hours' proofing at room temperature the next day.

8. Once the dough has proofed, you're ready to use it in your recipe.

If you prefer, you can use a stand mixer for the kneading (it's much easier on the hands!). Place the ingredients in the bowl in the order they are listed in the recipe method and fit the mixer with a dough hook. You'll only need to work the dough for 3 to 5 minutes on medium speed using a stand mixer.

savory shortcrust pastry
{ pâte brisée }

Makes enough for one
(10-inch/25 cm) tart shell

Prep time: 30 minutes

Chilling time: 1 hour

Bake time: 28 to 30 minutes
for a partially baked shell,
35 to 40 minutes for a fully
baked shell (see p. 170).

∽

INGREDIENTS

FOR THE PASTRY

1½ cups (225 g) all-purpose
flour

¼ teaspoon fine sea salt

½ cup (113 g) very cold
unsalted butter, cut into
½-inch (1 cm) cubes

1 large egg, lightly beaten

2 tablespoons ice-cold water

FOR BAKING

Butter, for greasing the pan

1 large egg, lightly beaten

Once you've mastered the technique for making this pastry, you've got an easy weeknight dinner up your sleeve! This pastry can be used to make quiche (p. 46), and once you know how to make a quiche, you have an excellent "clean out the fridge" type meal at your fingertips. Once you've made your shell, you can partially or fully bake it. Partially baking a tart shell is sometimes called "blind baking." We use this technique when the shell will be filled with wet ingredients and baked (like a quiche). Partial baking helps the pastry remain crispy as the filling bakes through (in the quiche recipe on p. 46 for example).

make the pastry:

1. Whisk the flour and salt in a large bowl. Add the cubed butter and, using your fingertips, lightly rub the butter into the flour until it resembles large breadcrumbs with some pieces the size of small peas. You can also use a pastry blender for this job.

2. Make a well in the middle of the flour mixture and add the egg. Using a wooden spoon, mix the egg into the flour until they are completely combined.

3. Add the water and mix until the dough is firm enough to form a ball when you press it together with your fingers—it might be a little crumbly, but shape the dough into a disk and wrap it tightly in plastic wrap.

4. Refrigerate for at least 1 hour, or up to 3 days in the fridge. You can also freeze the dough, tightly wrapped in plastic for up to 3 months. Thaw it overnight in the fridge before you roll and bake.

☺ Kids love working with pastry but they can sometimes be a little, shall we say, overly enthusiastic. Overworked pastry produces a tougher result and you risk losing the lovely flaky pastry that chunks of unworked butter will make. When I make pastry by hand with my boys' cooking club, the test to see whether they are overworking (i.e., squeezing) the dough is to take a look at their hands. If just their fingertips are covered in flour and butter, they are doing it right. If the palms of their hands are coated as well, it means they are squeezing the butter and flour, which will result in a tough pastry. We do the "hands up" check every so often when we make pastry—it keeps kids actively focused on what they are doing.

make a 10-inch (25 cm) pastry shell:

1. Lightly grease a 10-inch (25 cm) tart pan, even if it's a nonstick pan.
2. Remove the dough from the fridge, let it sit for a few minutes and roll it between two sheets of parchment paper until it's about 12 inches (30 cm) in diameter.
3. Carefully peel off the top layer of the parchment and place your tart pan upside down on the pastry disk. Place one hand underneath the dough and the other on the tart pan and flip it over so you have the tart pan on the bottom and the dough on top. Gently peel the remaining parchment paper off the dough and press the dough into the pan. If your dough breaks in places you should have enough overhang to patch things up. Make sure to press it into the edges of the pan with your fingertips.
4. Once the pastry is pressed into the pan, use a rolling pin to roll around the edges of the top of the pan to remove any extra pastry at the sides.
5. Refrigerate the pastry shell for 30 minutes.
6. Partially or fully bake the shell, depending on your recipe (see p. 170 for baking times).

I make this pastry in the food processor more often than not. It only takes a few pulses to cut the butter into the flour, and then a few more to incorporate the wet ingredients. So, it's much more efficient but much less fun for kids. If you want a flakier pastry, you'll need large as well as small chunks of butter in your pastry, and that is much easier to control when you make it by hand.

sweet shortcrust pastry
{ pâte sucrée }

Makes enough for one (10-inch/25 cm) tart shell; eight (6-inch/15 cm) individual galettes; or twenty (3-inch/ 7 cm) mini tart shells

Prep time: 30 minutes

Chilling time: 1½ hours

Bake time: 35 to 40 minutes for a fully baked shell

∽

INGREDIENTS

FOR THE PASTRY

1½ cups (225 g) all-purpose flour

¼ teaspoon fine sea salt

¼ cup (50 g) granulated sugar

½ cup (113 g) cold unsalted butter, cut into small cubes

1 large egg, lightly beaten

2 tablespoons heavy (35%) cream

FOR BAKING

Butter for greasing the pan

1 large egg, lightly beaten

Like the savory version of this pastry, this is an extremely versatile tart dough, and you can use it for all sorts of desserts—from simple recipes like the Mixed Berry Galettes (p. 123) or the Mini Jam Tarts (p. 74) to something a little more refined like the Strawberry Tart (p. 129). The possibilities for this are endless.

1. Whisk the flour, salt and sugar together in a large bowl. Add the cubed butter and, using your fingertips, lightly rub the butter into the flour until it resembles large breadcrumbs with some pieces the size of small peas. You can also use a pastry blender for this job.
2. Make a well in the middle of the flour mix and add the egg. Using a wooden spoon, mix the egg into the flour until they are completely combined.
3. Add the cream and mix until the dough is firm enough to form a ball when you press the mixture together with your fingers—it might be a little crumbly, but form the dough into a disk and wrap it tightly in plastic wrap.
4. Refrigerate for a minimum of 1 hour, or up to 3 days, in the fridge. You can also freeze the dough, tightly wrapped in plastic, for up to 3 months. Thaw it overnight in the fridge before you roll and bake.

make a 10-inch (25 cm) pastry shell:

1. Lightly grease a 10-inch (25 cm) tart pan, even if it's a nonstick pan.
2. Remove the dough from the fridge, let it sit for a few minutes and roll it between two sheets of parchment paper until it's about 12 inches (30 cm) in diameter.
3. Carefully peel off the top layer of the parchment and place your tart pan upside down on the pastry disk. Place one hand underneath the dough and the other on the tart pan and flip it over so you have the tart pan on the bottom and the dough on top. Gently peel the remaining parchment off the dough and press the dough into the pan. If your dough breaks in places you should have enough overhang to patch things up. Make sure to press it into the edges of the pan with your fingertips.

4. Once the pastry is pressed into the pan, use a rolling pin to roll around the edges of the top of the pan to remove any extra pastry at the sides.

5. Refrigerate the pastry shell for 30 minutes.

6. Partially or fully bake the shell, depending on your recipe (see p. 170 for baking times).

To partially bake a sweet or savory shortcrust pastry shell:

1. Preheat the oven to 375°F (190°C).
2. Remove the pastry shell from the fridge and prick the bottom lightly a few times with the tines of a fork.
3. Place a nonstick or lightly greased piece of aluminum foil or parchment paper over the top of the shell, making sure to cover it completely. Cover with baking beans or pie weights.
4. Bake for 25 minutes.
5. Remove the beans/weights and foil/parchment, and lightly brush the surface of the pastry with the beaten egg. Bake for a further 3 to 5 minutes.
6. Remove from the oven and let cool before following the instructions in your recipe.

To fully bake a sweet or savory shortcrust pastry shell:

1. Preheat the oven to 375°F (190°C).
2. Remove the pastry shell from the fridge and prick the bottom lightly a few times with the tines of a fork.
3. Place a nonstick or lightly greased piece of aluminum foil or parchment paper over the top of the shell, making sure to cover it completely. Cover with baking beans or pie weights.
4. Bake for 25 minutes.
5. Remove the beans/weights and foil/parchment, and lightly brush the surface of the pastry with the beaten egg. Bake a further 10 to 15 minutes until the pastry is golden.
6. Remove from the oven and let cool before following the instructions in your recipe.

rough puff pastry
{ pâte feuilletée rapide }

Makes enough for two large tarts, 40 Palmier Cookies, 12 Mini tartes Tatin and 1 Galette des rois

Prep time: 20 minutes

Chilling time: 1 hour

∽

INGREDIENTS

1¼ cups (187 g) all-purpose flour, plus extra for rolling

¼ teaspoon fine sea salt

½ cup (113 g) very cold unsalted butter, cut into 8 pieces

⅓ cup (80 mL) ice-cold water

All-purpose flour, for dusting

¼ cup (57 g) unsalted butter, frozen and grated (keep this in the freezer until you need it)

"Homemade puff pastry? Really?" I hear you ask. Really. I came across this method a few years ago, while perusing Clotilde Dusoulier's excellent Chocolate & Zucchini website. She referenced a technique used by Lucy Vanel of the Plum Lyon Teaching Kitchen that cut back on the fussy technique that real puff pastry calls for. No more making a *détrempe* (butter, flour and water) and encasing a flattened block of butter inside, rolling, folding and turning the dough umpteen times, then chilling between each turn. This recipe comes together in 15 to 20 minutes and once you've tried it you'll never buy store-bought again! You'll be able to use this in the Palmier Cookies (p. 77), *Mini tartes Tatin* (p. 127) and *Galette des rois* (p. 149).

1. Place the flour, the salt and then the cold butter pieces in the bowl of a food processor fitted with a metal blade. Pulse four to five times, until some of the butter is incorporated into the flour and some of it is still in pea-sized pieces.

2. Add the water and pulse three to four times, until the dough resembles cheese curds. If you gently squeeze the mix with your fingers, it should stick together. If you are not using a food processor, you can very gently mix the water in with a rubber spatula.

3. Tip the dough out onto a lightly floured surface and bring it together gently with your hands into the shape of a rough rectangle.

4. Lightly flour a rolling pin and roll the rectangle until it's 10 to 12 inches (25 to 30 cm) long and 4 to 6 inches (10 to 15 cm) wide. It will be around ½ inch (1 cm) thick.

5. Sprinkle the frozen butter onto the rectangle of pastry, making sure it's evenly distributed, and gently press it into the pastry with your fingertips.

6. Fold the top of the pastry to about two-thirds of the way down, then fold the bottom third up over the first fold. You might need a plastic bench scraper or spatula to help you scoop up the pastry if it's sticking a little.

As with other pastry recipes, you can rub the butter into the flour using your hands but it requires you to have very cold hands and to work quickly. I run my hands under cold water for a minute or two then dry them quickly and well before I start. If you're working with kids, it's perhaps better to have them focus on the rolling and folding aspect of this recipe, so use the food processor. If the dough is too warm to begin with, you won't end up with a flaky pastry, even if you work quickly on the rolling and folding part of the recipe.

7. Turn the block of pastry 90 degrees clockwise so the seam (the open ends of the pastry) is on your right. This rolling and folding is known as a "turn."

8. Repeat the flouring, rolling and folding process three more times (for a total of four turns). Make sure you brush the excess flour off the pastry and the rolling pin each time.

9. Wrap the pastry block tightly in plastic wrap and refrigerate for at least 1 hour or until you are ready to use it. The pastry can also be frozen for up to 1 month, wrapped tightly in plastic. Thaw in the fridge overnight before you use it.

choux pastry
{ pâte à choux }

Makes about 50 puffs or
20 éclairs

Prep time: 25 minutes

∽

INGREDIENTS

1 cup (250 mL) 2% milk

½ cup (113 g) unsalted butter,
cut into 4–6 small pieces

¼ teaspoon fine sea salt

1 cup (150 g) all-purpose flour

4 large eggs, at room
temperature

This versatile pastry can be used
to make *Chouquettes* (p. 61),
Gougères (p. 85), *Profiteroles*
(p. 139), *Éclairs* (p. 143) and the
Choux Puff Tower (p. 159).

Of all the pastry recipes I was afraid to try, choux might have been the scariest. It's the base for a whole bunch of sophisticated desserts as well as elegant appetizers, so I didn't think I could succeed in making this at home. In fact, this is one of the easiest and most forgiving pastry recipes you can make, but don't tell your friends. In just under an hour, you can create dozens of lovely choux puffs that you can fill and decorate with both sweet and savory options.

1. Bring the milk, butter and salt to a boil in a medium pot over medium-high heat.
2. Once the butter has melted, turn down the heat to medium-low and add the flour quickly, all at once.
3. Stir the mixture vigorously and continuously with a wooden spoon—it will come together fairly quickly, looking a little like mashed potatoes. Keep stirring over medium-low heat until it forms a smooth ball of dough, about 2 minutes. There might be a slight crust on the bottom of the pot, but that's fine!
4. Place the dough in a large clean glass or metal bowl (preferably one with high sides) and use a wooden spoon to break up the mixture a little to release the steam. Do not stir. Keep breaking up the mixture every 30 seconds or so, for a few seconds each time, for about 2 minutes so the dough loses some of its heat.
5. Once the steam rising from the pastry has more or less subsided, add one egg and stir even more vigorously than before using a wooden spoon. When you first add the egg, it will look like you've made a huge mistake—the mix will be sloppy and it might be hard to incorporate the egg into the pastry at first, but don't worry. If you keep stirring, your pastry will soon return to its mashed potato–like state.
6. Add another egg and stir vigorously until the pastry has come together again.
7. Continue adding the remaining eggs one at a time, stirring vigorously until the dough is soft, shiny and elastic.
8. Prepare the choux pastry according to the recipe you are using.

ACKNOWLEDGMENTS

They say it takes a village to raise a child. I say it takes a whole lot of people to write a children's cookbook. There are so many people I need to thank for making this project a reality:

The team at Appetite by Random House, especially Robert McCullough, who took a chance on a first-time author, and Zoe Maslow, who worked with me to make a beautiful book.

Kyla Zanardi, photographer extraordinaire, and Dara Sutin, exquisite food stylist. I can't thank you enough for your guidance throughout this project. I've learned so much from you both. Thank you for helping me find a way to express my vision of the book and for executing it so beautifully. We'll always have Lyon!

Houston Mauser and Savannah Onofrey, thank you for your tireless work behind the scenes on the Toronto photo shoots and for being there when I couldn't.

Lucy, Loïc and Ian Vanel. From that first meeting in Lyon in July 2016, when we wondered if it might be a good idea to do a photo shoot at the Plum Lyon Teaching Kitchen, to that crazy week in March 2017, when my team invaded your lives and home, you've been amazing. The beautiful images we shot in Lyon wouldn't have been possible without your generosity and energy. Ian, just when I needed some inspiration, you came along, just being yourself with your insightful comments, amazing playlist and gorgeous smile. You're my "French kid" forever!

The "kids in the French kitchen":

Members of the Petits Chefs cooking club. This book wouldn't exist without you. Special thanks to Kaden B., Gabe B., Sam C., Henry G., Drayden G., Jack G., Kabo L., Kasin L., Alex M., Charlie M., Jamie S., Spencer S. and David Z. who joined my experimental "help me test my recipes" club from January to March 2017. Thanks for answering all my questions and helping me write some of the recipes.

The boys in the Grade 4 class of 2016–2017, especially Finn B., Atticus T., James S., Drayden G., Charlie M., Zach L., Geoffrey W., Aidan A. and Peter T. Your French food research projects helped me so much with my book. Working with you all on your assignments was so much fun (and so delicious!).

The children who participated in the photo shoots in Lyon and Toronto: Violette, Gaspard, Ernest, Romy, Ian, Lisa, Jack, Finn, Sam, Henry and Oliver. Your patience and good humor made the photo shoots so easy and so much fun.

My chief recipe tester, Mary Catherine Anderson. A true friend (the kind who humors you as you send text after panicked text) from whom I've learned so much. You provided clarity and guidance and the book is so much better for your input. Thank you for measuring cup after cup of chopped vegetables when I just couldn't!

My recipe testers: Amanda L., Brian R. and Maddy, Carole N.-B., Carolyn W., Caron T. and Cian, Cathie G-S., Cathy B., Cathy I., Cecile C. and Cora, Ceri M., Dara G., Debbie S., Deborah P., Diane G., Dominique H., Emily C., Guillemette B., Hema R., Jacquie B. and Oliver, Janet S., Jennie R., Jennifer C., Jocie B., Jonathan B., Justin B., Karen H., Karina D., Kate H., Katie B., Laura McP. and Gwyneth, Lesli C-K., Lindsay Y., Lui M. and Luca, Luke R., Mary Luz M., Megan M., Melanie N. and Tara, Michelle C-W., Miranda R., Pam M., Rochelle R., Samantha V., Sanaz G., Sandy A-N., Savannah B., Simon C., Stephanie C., Stephanie E., Stephen B., Tami S., Terri B-S., Terri S., Thomas S., Trisha McC. Your feedback and questions made the recipes better. Your excitement at succeeding with "complicated recipes" made me smile.

The folks at Le Creuset Canada who provided some of the gorgeous cookware that appears throughout the book. You can't have a French cookbook without a few quintessentially French pieces, right?

Jan Scott, Mairlyn Smith, Jenn Bartoli, Julie Van Rosendaal and Alison Fryer. Your support and friendship have seen me through this process more than you could possibly know. You all inspire me every day.

Jennifer Greco. You were there as I fine-tuned the recipes that evening in Lyon in July 2016. Thank you for our early-morning (for me) text pep talks! Also, thank you for teaching me there aren't many problems that can't be sorted over a plate of French cheese!

Dorie Greenspan. My cheerleader extraordinaire. You taught me so much as I worked my way through *Around My French Table* during 2010–2015, and along the way we became friends. Your excitement and support for this project have been invaluable. Thank you for opening my eyes to the idea of French food being so doable for everyone, even kids!

Catherine Kirkland, who took a chance on me starting a cooking club in January 2010 and who always supports my schemes to incorporate cooking into French class.

My colleagues at Royal St George's College in Toronto. You sure make a girl and her baked goods feel loved! Special thanks to all the teachers who have assisted me with this club over the years, and the kitchen team for all their help with the club too.

My blog readers and followers. Thank you for seeing something in all those photos of little hands and posts about kids' cooking. Your support and virtual cheerleading have meant so much to me and, let's be honest, I wouldn't be writing a book if it wasn't for you!

My neighbors Steve, Linda, Orest and Lois. You tasted so much of this food when I was developing the recipes, and while your feedback wasn't always so useful ("Yum" "So good" "The best!"), it was encouraging.

Neil. Little did you know as you shouted "*Bonjour!*" at me from a rooftop in Casablanca in December 1999 what it would lead to. Thank you for supporting all my crazy, impossible dreams. And for providing wine as I worked.

INDEX

b17469156